THE
KING
of
COLOR

THE KING

of

COLOR

The Story of Pantone and the Man Who Captured the Rainbow

Lawrence Herbert
with Linda Mead

Published by
Lawrence Herbert

Printed in the United States of America.

Library of Congress Control Number: 2007939209 ISBN 978-0-578-44328-7

Contents

Acknowledgements

I am a very lucky man. I have been surrounded by colorful people and events that have gone into the making of this book.

To my children, I send my love, and a special thanks to Lisa, Vicky, and Richard, who helped drive the company and thus, this book. Well done, kids.

To those many hardworking Pantone employees, now and over the years, I offer my heartfelt appreciation and gratitude. I especially want to acknowledge Shellee Gero and Billy Chien, who have worked at my side through thick and thin.

To the originator of this project, Linda Mead, I send thanks for helping in the realization of this book.

Finally, I want to thank all of the designers, printers, marketing and advertising people, publishers, etc., who endorsed my universal Language of Color concept and found PANTONE Products useful throughout the years; I couldn't have done it without you.

Foreword

Pantone Chairman and CEO Lawrence Herbert didn't invent color, but he left many green with envy when he turned it into a lucrative business. Annually, billions of dollars worth of product makes use of the PANTONE Color Systems and trademarks. From the illusive rainbow sprang a multitude of big businesses in marketing, printing, electronics, cosmetics, home fashion, clothing and textile manufacturing, with Pantone playing a role in all.

Pantone is the protocol for color communication from designer to manufacturer to retailer to customer. Its technologies are embedded in the Stanley Tools on your workbench, the Kmart towels in your bathroom, the Mohawk carpeting in your living room, the Kellogg cereal box on your kitchen table, the Nike sneakers in your closet, the Barbie doll box on your daughter's shelf, the flying Microsoft windows icon, the Bank One card in your wallet, the Hallmark greeting card you received on your birthday, Pantone colored cell phones, even the jacket on this book. Every year, Pantone and its licensees in more than 100 countries sell products carrying the PANTONE Mark of color, even the Pantone Brand Name.

The fact is that everything we come in contact with today, whether a magazine we read, the car we drive, or the clothes we wear, somehow relies on the color industry — an industry born out of myth, lore and tradition dating back to prehistoric man. And perhaps this is where the story of Pantone really begins.

Pictures and color provided one of the first means of communicating our ideas and needs without words. Colored substances extracted from the earth, along with charcoal from spent fires, created the visuals on Neolithic cave walls and in human rituals. One of those first colors, red ochre, to this day maintains its close association with the powerful symbolism of life-giving blood. In ancient times, Neolithic man buried his dead by painting the body in red ochre, thus signifying the reenactment of birth and offering life-giving powers. Perhaps, even before the ancient Egyptians, this was a initial telling of rebirth and afterlife. The Bible portrays Adam as having been fashioned from red clay or red earth, which clearly resembles the red ochre and signifies the lifeblood. Not surprisingly, the Hebrew words for blood and red have the same origin: "dm" meaning red and "dom" meaning blood.

By ancient times, natural color substances became a commodity sought by many, but reserved for very few. Blue and green substances, though similarly derived from the Earth, appear to date only to ancient Egypt, around 2500 B.C. Stone Age man most likely lacked a pigment resource for blue and green where he resided, but theories also surfaced regarding his inability to discern between these two colors. The Egyptians, however, mined and crushed precious blue lapis lazuli and azurite to create the coloring meant only for god-like status. Blue tinted royal eyelids depicted the embodiment of gods like Amun and adorned the royal graves in the Valley of the Kings — most notably, the sarcophagus mask made for Tutankhamen in gold and lapis.

Purple, too, came to hold an especially high place for royalty. As early as 2000 B.C., the ancient Greeks in Tyre began extracting the purpora dye from the mucous glands of decaying mollusks. Legend has it that Heracles' dog discovered and began chewing on the snail-like creatures while walking with his master along the Levantine Coast. The dog's purple-stained mouth gave Heracles the idea to dye a robe for King Phoenix, who was so impressed with the outcome that he declared purple the color of royals and decreed death as the punishment for anyone else irreverent enough to bare the color.

So important was the high quality, rich color as a symbol of lineage, that one had to be born in a purple birthing chamber to be considered a legitimate heir to the throne. Only then could a royal be bequeathed the signature name like that given to Constantine VII (904-959 A.D.), also known as Constantine Poxphyrogenitus (purple born).

The fact that it took some four million rotting shellfish to produce one pound of pure purple dye made it a commodity as costly as gold. Even if commoners had been allowed to use the color, they would not have been able to afford it. Ironically, the rank, intense-smelling concoction that infused the skin of the royal dyers, and followed them wherever they went, making them societal outcasts, also tinted the lips and eyelids of Empirical Romans.

If it had not been the demise of Constantinople in 1453 that caused the fall of the Roman Empire, it might well have been the stench of Tyrian purple. Regardless of the cause, with the Empire's fall came the fading of the purple dye industry. Left were less expensive, less intense versions made from lichen and madder — pale imitations that the populace could afford. Natural Tyrian purple still exists today, but it commands a vast sum. Fortunately for us, the synthetic dye industry — brought about in the mid-nineteenth century by William Perkin's discovery of the aniline-based dye, mauveine, while searching for a malaria cure — offers an inexpensive alternative.

Limited to hues derived from nature's minerals, plants and creatures, color in ancient times imparted important information and set the tone for the future of color. Whether a reflection of our beliefs, heritage, clan, religion or economic times, innumerable histories steeped in religion and culture have come to dictate color's use and meaning. To an Asian, for example, white is the color used in mourning — the Japanese phrase for funeral meaning "white event." Yet, black signals mourning in other cultures. Either way, in most cultures, it is generally agreed that white symbolizes purity, innocence and perfection. That explains why babies don white christening dresses, women marry in white veils and, for Asians, the dead are guided to a pure, peaceful place shrouded in white.

Over the years, many groups and organizations have adopted colors to identify their family or business. For example, Scottish clans distinguished themselves by the unique plaids woven from their chosen family colors, dating back to Scotland's King James III in 1471. Evidently, the Celts had used striped and checked material for thousands of years. The Scoti, who settled Western Scotland from the fifth and sixth centuries onward and eventually gave the whole country its name, are said to have used it to signify rank. Perhaps the earliest clan tartan, a 3rd Century natural brown and white checked fabric, was unearthed at a Roman-built wall near Falkirk.

Nations, too, have defined themselves with color. Every nation uses one or a combination of the colors red, yellow, green, blue, black and white in its flag. The five Olympic rings on a white background, first presented during the Antwerp Games in 1920, have come to represent the five continents on a sea of peace. Each color means something to a people, a nation, or a religion.

When Moses ascended Mount Horeb (Sinai), he "saw the God of Israel: and there was under his feet as it were a paved work of a sapphire stone, and as it were the body of heaven in *his* clearness."[1] Thus, Israel fashions its flag in blue, which, according to late Prime Minister Golda Meier, reflects the sky, and as Leatrice Eiseman, director of the Pantone Color Institute®, reports, "In the human

---

[1] *The Holy Bible, King James Version, American Bible Society New York, 1999.*

THE KING *of* COLOR

mind, we always connect the color blue with the sky on a good day." Most Muslim-populated (Islamic) countries fly the color green to show reverence for Muhammad, who apparently wore a green cloak. The use of green actually dates back to ancient Arabic times and the nomadic lifestyle of seeking eternal oases. The Koran reads, "As to those who believe and do good works…for them are prepared gardens [green] of eternal abode." Kuwait's most recent flag, adopted in 1961, for instance, regales green as symbolic of "our spring homes" in a poem by Safie Al-Deen Al-Hali. Used throughout the world from Pan-African nations to Ireland and others, its name derived from the old Teutonic root 'grô,' meaning to grow, green reflects the land, nature, growth, hope and faith.

Yellow, the brightest of the basic colors, is also the least used primary color in national flags. An anciently derived color, it spoke of light and sun, ordained kings and priests throughout the Middle

East and Asia, and remains sacred to Brahmanism, Buddhism and Confucianism. A symbol of Empirical China, commoners were not allowed to wear yellow until modern times. Often referred to as gold, it poses as a color associated with riches. The flag of Zimbabwe, for example, utilizes yellow bands to refer to the wealth of minerals in the country.

But just what is color, that mysterious contrivance whose rainbow's end eludes our reach? Essentially, color is all in our mind. Received by the eye and interpreted by the brain, it exists only because of light.

"What do you need for color?" remarks Pantone's Ken Niepokoy, vice president, manufacturing & color technology. "Light and an observer."

Painters glorified canvasses, and rainbows splayed their storm-laden colors long before Isaac Newton introduced his color theory to the world one day in 1665. In fact, Newton didn't explain color or light so much as the refraction of light into color bands. His conclusion: light bends through the prism the same way it must bend through raindrops to create the colored rays of the rainbow. Two centuries later, Scottish physicist James Maxwell revealed the connection.

Light is energy — the only visible form of energy. The sun's light reaches us and we see it. Other forms of electromagnetic energy, though a part of our everyday lives, remain invisible to us: ultraviolet, infrared, X-rays, microwave, radar, TV and radio frequencies, and brain waves (yes, thinking is an electromagnetic vibration, as is seeing). The color spectrum falls within this visible range of light, and each color dances to its own beat, vibrating at a different rate. When the different colored bands traverse in sync, they absorb into one another to form white (i.e., the lack of color). The colors we see, whether in a painting or the sky, are those frequencies that get through to us. Bounce light off an object, whether an orange or a painting of an orange, and those rays reflected off the object render its color.

Colors combine in two distinctive manners and use two different systems of primaries. First, pigment, or any pigment-based medium, works with the more commonly known primaries — red, yellow and blue. Conceivably, the great masters such as Michelangelo, Raphael or Vermeer, could have created their masterpieces by mixing just these three colors. The second system, light, whose primary colors are red (long wavelength), green (mid-range) and blue (short), provides the means by which we see color, including any pigment or paint-related media. So, when we mix pigments to create color, let's say red and yellow to make orange, we still see the resulting color by means of the reflection of light.

Finally, why do we perceive a lemon, or a painting of a lemon, as yellow? "The color of the object illuminated partakes of the color of that which illuminates it," explained Leonardo da Vinci over 500 years ago.

The eye is constructed with photoreceptors (rods and cones) to

THE RED, YELLOW AND GREEN TRAFFIC LIGHT

*The traffic light originated as a railroad signal
designation system that used color filters over lights.
Red meant stop, green meant caution, and white, or no
color, meant proceed. When a green or red filter
failed to drop, leaving white, however, a few too many
accidents occurred. So the color system was changed
to our modern day usage. Considered the invention of
Garrett Morgan, who acquired the patent in 1923,
the first three-color, four-way traffic light system was
invented around 1920 by a Detroit policeman, William
Potts, and installed in both Detroit and New York City.*

receive all light-energy wavelengths, and when received together, perceives them as white. When any of the wavelengths is missing (or has been absorbed by an object), we see color as those remaining wavelengths reflect back to us. As all light wavelengths hit the lemon (or a painting or photograph of a lemon, though created in the red-yellow-blue pigment system), the blue wavelength (opposite of yellow) is absorbed and the red and green wavelengths bounce off. In the light system (Red-Green-Blue), these two reflected wavelengths combine to create yellow. (Think of a streetlight Red-Yellow-Green). The rods and cones in our eyes vibrate with these wavelengths and send a message to our brain that says 'Yellow.'

Although the science of color can be complicated, the business is simple: Pantone owns the spectrum. Not the colors themselves, of course. Frequencies of light are free to the eye of the beholder, as color essentially rests in the mind. But Pantone has made a business out of capturing and copyrighting the spectrophotometric formulas for everything from "stop sign red" to thousands of other shades, tones and tints imaginable. The firm codifies each hue — and the recipe for reproducing it — with a PANTONE Number, and then sells those codes in color chip books, swatch binders, fan decks (so-called because they open like Chinese fans) and for technology.

In other words, it's a Pantone universe.

The core of that universe is a building set in the bland outreaches of Carlstadt, New Jersey. Long asphalt thoroughfares of nondescript commercial buildings look out over weed-choked, salty marshlands just beyond The Meadowlands Sports Complex, home of the New York Giants, and five miles from the bright lights of Manhattan. An immaculate brick building set on verdant manicured grounds, and located amidst the clothing, leather goods and paper manufacturers that share this thoroughfare, Pantone broadcasts its name in two-foot tall rainbow colors.

Step inside the 80,000 square foot headquarters of this forty-plus-year-old company, and you will find quiet, unimaginative offices on the second floor — save for the Oz-like change of wall color that occurs from hallway to hallway, accompanied by oversized, matching PANTONE Color Chips. Follow the color-swathed walls, from Pale

Mauve (PANTONE 15-1607), Canyon Clay (PANTONE 16-1431), Hemp (PANTONE 14-0721) and Blush (PANTONE 15-1614) to Italian Straw (PANTONE 13-0917), Whisper White (PANTONE 11-0701) and Cloud Blue (PANTONE 14-4306), and you'll wind your way to the Wizard who captured the rainbow: Chairman and CEO Lawrence Herbert, known to family, friends and colleagues as Larry and to employees as "LH."

On the cavernous factory floor below, thunderous printing presses pound out vibrant rows of multi-colored stripes on reams of coated, matte and uncoated white card stock. While the aver-age press prints four to ten colors at a time, the newest incarnation of the split fountain invention Larry originated forty-five years ago applies up to thirty-six colors simultaneously. Cut and neatly arranged in stacks, the signature seven-stripe color cards, produced at a rate of thousands of sheets per hour, await shuffling before shipping.

In a nearby lab, a computer commands dozens of different dyes to surge through clear plastic tubing and into steel canisters, where, once blended and checked, are transferred to tubs awaiting bolts of virgin white cotton fabric. Each color-charged bolt joins 1,925 others as part of the PANTONE Textile Color System®. The swatches, arranged chromatically, 35 to a page, form the quintessential textbook intended for fashion, home furnishings and cosmetic industry use.

Over in the Color Technology Laboratory, a color scientist uses a spectrophotometer to measure the amount of light energy reflected by a particular color and logs the complex data set, known as the spectral curve, into a computer. Down the hall, in a neutral gray room devoid of décor, Color Standards Laboratory technicians sit under special daylight-simulating viewing lights to ensure color accuracy in textile swatches, printed matter, inks and plastics for its clients that number in the millions.

"Color is so subjective," admits graphic designer and artist Milton Glaser. "Everybody's eye is structured differently and no one sees color the same. It's a complex issue." That is why some may refer to the distinctive Tiffany packaging (chosen by the company's founder back in 1853 because it was a favorite color of Empress Eugenie, wife of Napoleon III) as green, while others, including David Lodestro of Tiffany & Company's advertising production department, assure us that it is blue.

In response to the inherent subjectivity of color perception, Pantone instituted a scientific approach. As eye structures vary and absorb the Red-Green-Blue wavelengths differently, every technician must pass a battery of visual acuity tests on a regular basis: from the Ishihara Color Blindness Test to the HVC Color Aptitude Test.

More succinctly put by Donkey in the movie SHREK, "Blue flowers, red thorns! Blue flowers, red thorns! Blue flowers, red thorns! Oh, this would be so much easier if I weren't color blind!" As it is known that women experience color blindness far less often than men, women more readily occupy this technical position.

In another lab, a batch of metallic ink samples glitter like fool's

IN THE EYE OF THE BEHOLDER

Color Blind, *the term generally used to refer to individuals who cannot differentiate between certain colors, first came to note when English Chemist John Dalton published a scientific paper after realizing his own color blindness. Mostly seen in men, several forms of this deficiency appear: red/green, yellow/blue, and monochromasy — the complete absence of color. The latter rare genetic defect, in which the individual sees objects in black, white and gray appears in every 1 of 30,000 individuals, and seems to be associated with a limited gene pool. Such is the case in Oliver Sachs book,* The Island of the Color Blind, *where the South Pacific natives of Pingelap Island have a one in 12 rate of total color blindness resulting from inbreeding.*

gold in small round dishes, awaiting quality control analysis. Sitting not far away, a game-like device, the Fade-o-meter, helps determine the rapidity of color loss. "If we wanted to know what our colors would look like on Mars," jests Niepokoy, "we could simulate color fading on Mars."

Inside a door marked "Electronic Color Systems," programmers manipulate color data for digital printers made by different companies such as Hewlett-Packard and Xerox. That way, when a user specifies Cerulean blue in a PANTONE Color on the computer screen, each printer spews out the identical shade that looks like Cerulean blue, instead of sapphire, cobalt or periwinkle.

Today, the business of color is big business, and none is bigger than Pantone. Under Larry's wizardry, Pantone has become a major contributor to — and the benchmark for — all industries. The world's leading printers and ink manufacturers use the copyrighted PANTONE MATCHING SYSTEM®. Advertising agencies, marketing and branding companies request specially formulated corporate colors for their clients. Fashion and interior design moguls use the PANTONE VIEW Colour Planner for their seasonal forecasting of trends. Retailers from the Gap to Kmart rely on Pantone's swatches as easy, understandable standards for production in far-off places.

Computer color graphics and printers are clearer, cleaner and more precise when imbedded with PANTONE Codes, and remain that way with huey™, an award-winning gizmo that color corrects a computer monitor. No computer monitors are alike when they leave the factory and over time, the colors they display will fade. Huey, when placed directly on the screen with its little suction cups, measures the light-emitted colors from the computer screen, evaluates, adjusts and restabilizes the colors in less than one minute. Huey then creates a profile for the computer. In partnership with Radius Technologies, the huey precursor — a bulky and expensive brick-sized device — has been transformed into a finger-length, easy-to-set-up up gadget at a remarkably consumer-friendly retail price.

Pantone's arm reaches to an unimaginable list of industries

companies and products, from Christie's Auction House to Ford Motor Company, *Men's Health* magazine to Estée Lauder Fragrances, Puma sports to the NFL, Abercrombie & Fitch to Gap, Burberry to J. Crew, UPS to Fed Ex, Coca-Cola to Smirnoff Vodka, Ben & Jerry's Ice Cream to Oscar Mayer, Amgen Pharmaceuticals to Gojo Skin Care, to name a very few. All have been touched by Pantone.

Pantone can boast millions of customers around the world because its products remain essential to anyone who needs to communicate color unambiguously. Over four decades, Pantone has become the color genome for graphic and industrial design, printing, publishing, packaging, manufacturing, fashion, interiors and architecture. Imagine, for example, a graphic designer creating a new logo for a client. She designs the logo on a computer screen using software embedded with PANTONE Colors. She prints out the logo on a color printer that is licensed by Pantone. She opens her PANTONE MATCHING SYSTEM Color book, tears out a postage-stamp size color chip in the exact shade of the new logo and attaches the chip to a proof for the printer (who will print the final product using ink from a Pantone-licensed ink maker). The result: the perfect blue on the Pillsbury box of cake mix in your cupboard (PANTONE 286) or the perfect warm, deep, rich, welcoming Chinese red for New York's Museum of Modern Art, replacing the original PANTONE 485 red used since 1984, which seemingly was too connected to the Russian Constructivism art movement.

That's a far cry from how business and industry used to specify the colors they required. When Lenox, the maker of china, dinnerware and giftware, required a color match for a new product, the company would send its designers on exhaustive searches for a reference piece in just the right hue. When they finally stumbled upon a flea market find that matched the color they had in mind, they would smash the item into pieces and ship the fragments to overseas contractors to use as a physical color reference. Now, Lenox designers choose an opaque or transparent plastic chip from the PANTONE Plastics Color System™, order multiple chips in the desired color, and send them to production facilities. The system is faster, cheaper, more efficient, and ensures a literal clone of product color among all of its factories.

In other words, it's a better way to communicate. Around the time Larry introduced the PANTONE MATCHING SYSTEM, the General Foods Corporation in-plant printing facility experienced problems with color matching. Most of the short run promotional literature required matching special colors, and unless they were standard and straight from the can, the pre-Pantone hit-and-miss method of mixing the inks became time-consuming and expensive. The manager of the department, recently apprised of the Pantone System, implemented its use. "What we've given the world is a common language for color specification, which never existed before," boasts Larry. Esperanto may have never caught on as a universal second language, but Pantone has.

Foreword

A single man transformed Pantone from a small business into a color empire. A man whose ideas coursed so ahead of the times, he had to create the learning curve and then convince others to join. His uncanny knack for hiring and managing passionate people who, if cut would likely bleed in multi-color, also propelled Pantone to its zenith. Because of his non-conventional vision and marketing talent, Lawrence Herbert will forever be known as the man who captured the rainbow and made it his.

Mere colour, unspoiled by
meaning, and unallied
with definite form, can speak
to the soul in a thousand
different ways.

— Oscar Wilde

From Press to Promise

While throngs filled Manhattan's sun-drenched Fifth Avenue to display pastel-hued spring finery for the Sunday Easter Parade in April 1962, Larry Herbert had other things on his mind. Tomorrow was a workday. The past week had been short but arduous: taxes had been due last Monday, Passover had begun on Wednesday night and, by Friday, Larry had confirmed with the company accountant that the business was slowly being drained by his partners in Pantone Press, Mervyn and Jesse Levine. The brothers were taking their profits from the printing side of the business to fund their floundering display business. The situation strained the press's coffers and Larry's patience. His options were clear. Still, he needed a sympathetic ear. He would discuss the alternatives with his friend and carpool mate, Elsie Williamson.

Each day the carpool routine commenced at 8 a.m. when Sol, Jim, Belmont, Elsie and Larry drove from New City, New York, to Manhattan. The forty-minute drive, down Route 304, across Route

59 to the Palisades Interstate Parkway, over the steely George Washington Bridge and onto the West Side Highway, deposited the five-some at 57th Street and Eleventh Avenue. The carpoolers let Elsie Williamson, assistant treasurer of International Flavors and Fragrances, off first. They continued south dropping the rest at the final destination — 34th Street. During their travel time together, Jim, in the stock transfer department of General Motors, and Belmont, a textile designer with Burlington Industries, would chat, while Sol, a freelance writer, would sleep.

Larry and Elsie always sat next to one another and discussed their businesses as they drove through the pastoral greenery dotted with brazen yellow forsythia, and then crossed the Hudson River into the drab unyielding forest.

For Larry, the garment district teemed with Technicolor® life: each season's palette scurried across the streets on rolling racks then seamlessly disappeared. He noticed the changes in colors from season to season — soft pastels, bold bright colors, and subtler dark shades came and went. That was his business. He had worked at Pantone Press as a pressman and color matcher since 1956. In the prior year, 1961, his money-making printing innovations had finally secured him half ownership in the press.

Every Monday through Friday, the four men took turns driving since Elsie had never learned how. This week would be different. Larry called his three other carpool buddies, Sol, Jim and Belmont, on Sunday night and asked them to drive into Manhattan without

NAVY BLUES

Navy blue, a deep color closely resembling black, conveys,
along with many other highly saturated shades of blue,
a sense of authority, strength and resilience. Used by
Pict warriors (Scots), who dyed their skin blue and went
into battle naked to terrify their Roman opponents[2]
(who themselves wore red cloth to hide any bleeding and
therefore seem immortal), it was first introduced by the
Royal Navy in 1748. Since then, the deep ocean color
has garnered favor with navies throughout the world.

him and Elsie. He would pick up Elsie to talk to her alone.

Reminiscences of newness clung to the rich red leather interior of Larry Herbert's 1962 navy blue Cadillac Sedan de Ville, a car he cherished. It brought with it a sense of power and accomplishment.

Since acquiring half ownership in Pantone Press, he had been able to afford some of the finer things he so longed for, including a new car. He remembered his father Harry's first car in 1939 with fondness, but it had been a ten-year-old black and brown-roofed boxy Essex. Henry Ford had quipped in those early auto-making days, that people could have any color they wanted "as long as it's black." The pastel pinks, yellows, aquas, and two-toned cars stretching across

---

[2] *Ball, Philip, "Seeing Red...and Yellow...and Green...and," Natural History, March 2002*

America's highways, so fresh in the 1950s, spoke of softer times, optimism and renewal. Those same colors, saturated and refined for boldness, would define the 1960s.

As he pulled up to the curb of Elsie's Valley Cottage home, Sammy Davis, Jr. wailed the last lines of "What Kind of Fool Am I?" Larry turned the radio off as Elsie got in and closed the door behind her. Twenty-five or thirty years Larry's senior, Elsie had amassed great wealth in the stock market, inherited extensive coin and stamp collections and even acquired Amelia Earhardt's last flying suit. She and her husband, a vice president of the Beechnut Corporation, had no children on whom to dote, so Larry had assumed that role. He even helped them with their occasional household projects.

A good friend and confidante for nearly five years, Elsie listened intently to the young, driven Herbert, understood his yearning and, perhaps, knew his career path even before he did. As a service industry, printing stood between the manufacturer and the consumer. But Larry had never accepted himself as just a printer. His commitment to color separated him from others. Color drove his work just as the growth of consumerism drove color. At no time was this more evident than during the booming '50s, as symbolized in the "Think Pink" lyrics of the 1957 Audrey Hepburn film *Funny Face:*

Banish the black, burn the blue, and bury the beige!
From now on girls…
Think pink! Think pink! when you shop for summer clothes.

Think pink! Think pink! if you want that quel-que chose.
Red is dead, blue is through,
Green's obscene, brown's taboo.
And there is not the slightest excuse for plum or puce
— or chartreuse.
Thine pink, think pink
Think pink, think pink![3]

Larry's world had embraced color. The silent language substantiated economic good times. In a voice all its own, it reflected a people's character as it tacitly cajoled their purse strings.

Elsie understood Larry and understood his world. But did he think she would understand the notion that now consumed him? After the usual monosyllabic "morning" greeting, Larry anxiously dove into discussion.

"Elsie, I've been working on a system which I think could revolutionize the printing industry. I've been playing with it in my head for a while. It's a color standardization system that would allow everyone — ink manufacturers, printers, graphic designers — to designate colors by codes backed by an ink formula for the printers to reference," he told her.

A first for the printing industry, color standardization for the textile dye industry had been pioneered as early as 1915 by Margaret

---

[3] *Funny Face: Music: George Gershwin; lyrics: Ira Gershwin; Book: Fred Thompson and Paul Gerard Smith; from the 1957 film Funny Face.*

A COLOR BY ANY OTHER NAME

Though we are all capable of seeing over seven million colors, our languages, social conditioning and cultural surroundings limit us to naming a small fraction of these colors. Many languages, for example, use a single term to identify blue and green rather than distinguishing between the two,[4] whack is ironic since green gives us the widest range of distinguishable hues of all the colors in the spectrum.

Hayden Rourke, who formed the Textile Color Card Association of the United States to systematize the hues adopted by the clothing industry. To name the 92 colors of that time, Mrs. Rourke sent out thousands of questionnaires to the fashion industry, tabulated the results and issued a list. Though Rourke's system managed to identify colors and color trends, in this case during the depths of World War II, formulas for their reproduction were not part of the equation.

By 1940, Rourke's new list had grown to 200 fashion colors gathered from trends around the globe, and dispensed to apparel, cosmetics, furniture and automobile subscribers. While the world

[4] *The Color Blue: A Psychophysical Explanation for a Linguistic Phenomenon*

battled, Mrs. Rourke stated "...the only effect the war has had on colors is to make them gayer. France indulged in drab tones for the last war. Today it senses the value of color psychology. We need vivid shades to counterbalance the sobriety in the air."[5]

Other color systems, based on scientific visual perception theories in the nineteenth and early twentieth centuries, had made their way around the world. One such theory, revived from German physiologist Ewald Hering's color theory of opposing colors, was resurrected in Sweden in the 1930s by Dr. Tryggve Johansson, who developed a 'natural color system' illustrated by 600 color samples. None of these systems, however, was formulated for point of reference or reproduction. That's what truly set Larry's idea apart.

"This new color system would give the end-user consistency," he explained to Elsie. "I can't tell you how many times printing jobs have to be carefully watched on press, or thrown out when the color goes wrong. With my system, I can be in Michigan and choose a particular red, let's say, by a code number for my printers in New York and Hong Kong, and each would print the exact same color using the ink formula. No more matching paint chips. No more eyeballing color, pulling proofs and changing the job on press. It will all be scientific, not to mention enormously convenient."

Larry knew all too well how badly such a system was needed. Indeed, conflicts with the Levines — with whom he was now

---

[5] *Colors Named So All Could Identify Them: A Pioneer's Path Ends in Standardization by Adelaide Handy, NYT; May 19, 1940; page 52.*

partnered but who still commissioned print work for their display business — had triggered the idea. As a result, though Larry's color precision was always dead on, the same couldn't be said of his working relationship with the two brothers. Color charts produced for Jaguar nearly brought them to blows. To avoid a bleed-through situation when one color runs into another and creates a third unwanted color, Larry set the press up to run every third color in the fountain. This simply meant having to run the sheets through the press that much more often. On the last pass, instead of printing gray, which was the essential color, Larry had accidentally laid down blue.

"How are we going to fix this mess?" shrieked one of the Levine brothers.

"Don't worry," said Larry. "It's not as bad as it seems. We may not have to throw the job out."

"I'll be back," replied Levine. "See what you can do."

Larry concocted a color that would overprint and block out the blue, effectively resulting in the exact shade of gray needed, but the tension surrounding the situation cast a shadow on Larry's patience and goodwill.

Larry cringed every time he had to run a job for their advertising agency, which at the time was the parent company to Pantone Press. The brothers were critical and indecisive. Each project came with a dose of production heartburn. They would give Larry a color to match, and he would produce it. They would accept the proof of the job showing the color accuracy, but later decide, while on full press run, that it wasn't what they had okayed, declaring they hadn't seen the correct version or that Larry wasn't printing what they had approved. There was always an argument.

Finally, Larry uttered the words, "This would be a lot easier if we could control the color formulas." He further thought, *Why don't they just come up with a number for reference purposes? There wouldn't be any of the back and forth while on press. Pick a number that is a press proven color, match the number, run it and deliver it.*

It took just a second for the thought to register. That was it!

Rarely, if ever, has a solution been quite as timely.

The world teetered on the verge of a color revolution. By the early 1960s, the printing industry ran amuck in color, a fact that did not elude Larry. Turquoise and poodle pink faded away. In place of the '50s washed-out colors, an array of vibrant pinks, oranges and yellows emerged on the scene as "hot colors," while navy remained a solid, steadfast, conservative choice. Women sported bouffant, pale blond hair, and emulated Jacqueline Kennedy in their dress. The world, with its changing generational attitudes and new ideas, would soon turn an industry on its head and spawn ultra brights and neons. That would further complicate matters for a printing industry already challenged by the increasing and shifting commercial use of color. Since every printer bought ink from various sources and mixed its own colors, color matching was a hit-and-miss proposition. Requesting lemon yellow could yield shades from pale butter to gold. Coral meant anything from deep pink to orange. There was no industry standard. Put in a position to compete against color TV for advertising dollars, Madison Avenue, which relied heavily on color print media, scrapped jobs time after time for color inaccuracy.

Color application was the future, Larry recognized.

Advertisers now demanded photographic quality realism in print, and product clarity pushed to the limits. Prior print advertising that showcased merchandise, though produced in full color, had mostly been renderings. The dress at Lord & Taylor's, the Ipana toothpaste, even the Kodak film we were urged to buy, had all been depicted largely by drawings rather than color photos.

1960s color TV engaged advertisers to reflect American life, creatively presenting the decade's central issues: "environmental concerns as reflected by the Great Society programs of the Johnson administration, the Vietnam War, the Civil Rights movement, the burgeoning 'youth culture,' the women's movement and the sexual revolution."[6] Actors and singers who took up causes for the American Cancer Society (John Wayne) and the American Heart Association (Pearl Bailey, Patricia Neal) juxtaposed the Saturday morning cartoon commercials pushing Fruit Loops, Crispy Critters, Fruit Stripe gum or any number of sugared products. Appeals went out to moms to buy the newest brand of washers, dryers and refrigerators, and dads to covet a new family car. Oh, and don't forget to pick up Pall Mall cigarettes and Alka Seltzer on the way home! Life, reports the same

[6] *Karr Collection Television Commercials: Introduction; Library of Congress*
   http://www.loc.gov/rr/mopic/findaid/karr/karr1.html

guide, is "captured through use of jump cuts, montage editing, innovative lighting, 'mod' fashions, psychedelic graphics, and diverse music sound tracks — techniques later found in the music videos of the MTV era."[7]

Realism and drama forced the print media to compete for the dollars. That meant that print quality had to play catch up. Ink manufacturers, however, had no reason to collaborate or work together. They were plentiful, each vying for the printer's business and each marketing their inks with their own specially-created color book. They were in competition with one another, and as long as printers selected their products, they made money. Not much else mattered. Quality control was only a singular affair. The fact that end-users couldn't achieve the same quality or colors from one printer to another just wasn't their concern.

Nevertheless, it was a constant headache for every printer and in particular, challenged Larry.

Elsie had previously heard about Larry's difficulties with his partners, his frustration with opportunities that had presented themselves, and he was unable to seize. She had been generous with her time and help and had become a good and close friend. He had to take a chance.

"I have spoken with a number of people in the industry about the matching system idea and think it will be well-accepted," he

---

[7] *Karr Collection Television Commercials: Introduction; Library of Congress.*
http://www.loc.gov/rr/mopic/findaid/karr/karr1.html

THE KING of COLOR

explained to Elsie. "My problem is that I don't want to give it to Pantone. It's mine and I don't want to make any more money for them. I've spoken to the company accountant, and I think I can buy out the Levine's half."

"What makes you think so, Larry?"

"Well, I already talked them into making me half partner in the press without my having to spend a dime, didn't I?" he chortled, remembering how his threatening to quit had forced their hand. "They're hurting and need cash. If they don't go for it, I'll leave and develop the system on my own. Besides, I've been running-the printing side of things and have built up the business while they have been sitting by and pulling money out for their losing display business. I can sustain the business with print jobs until I can get them on board with the new system."

Larry Herbert continued to explain why he could get the Levine brothers to sell. Pantone, Inc., the display company, was on the verge of bankruptcy and an infusion of $30,000, according to the accountant, would solve their immediate problem. He felt strongly that they had to take an offer. If Elsie was willing to put up the capital, he concluded, she would become a fifty percent partner and run the financial side while he ran the business. Larry punctuated his pitch with a promise. He would pay her back in a year. But if she could not lend him the money, he added, he understood.

As Larry began to pull over to drop off Elsie at her office, she directed him to continue on, then to turn left on Eleventh Avenue and park in front of Chemical Bank.

"Come with me," she commanded as he opened the door for her.

With nothing more said between them, Larry escorted Elsie into the bank where the vice president greeted her. While the two exchanged niceties, Larry wondered what would follow.

"This is Mr. Herbert. I want you to issue a cashier's check to him for $50,000."

Stunned, Larry said nothing until they exited the bank. He slid the check inside his jacket pocket and placed his right hand over the outside area to hear the paper crinkle.

"No paperwork between us?" he questioned.

"None. This is a no-interest loan, Larry. You will either buy the company or you won't. Either way, I know you will make this thing happen. I will see you after work," she concluded, raising her hand, palm out in a silencing gesture. Then, sweeping her fingers fro to shoo him away, she turned and walked around the corner to her office on 57th Street.

It wasn't until 1970, when Larry decided to take his company public, that he would find out why she had been so generous.

During a visit with Elsie at her home on Babbling Brook Road, the two sat casually in her living room with a drink. He held out a piece of paper and began to speak, "Elsie, I wanted to give you this because of how you helped me get things going," and handed her a stock certificate for 25,000 shares of Pantone. Elsie held her hands out to receive the gift, then pressed it back into Larry's. "I don't want it," she replied before finally explaining why she had loaned Larry the money. She had been lucky enough to leave Germany before World War II began. Still, what happened to the Jews in her native country haunted her and, as a German, she couldn't help feeling that all Germans shouldered some responsibility. Helping Larry, a Jew, was her way of making amends. Her only request to Larry was that he someday find a way to help others. She wanted nothing else in return.

Larry knew none of this the day she handed him that check. Stunned at the turn of events, he simply couldn't believe his luck. When he settled into his office at 461 Eighth Avenue, he drew a huge breath and patted the pocket that held the check. It wasn't a dream. The crinkle of paper was still there. He called upstairs to see if Jesse Levine was in his office in the display division he headed. Jesse answered the phone.

Larry made an offer that afternoon. In a brief meeting, Larry told Jesse that he wanted to buy the press, he wanted nothing to do with the ailing display division, but was prepared to cover their debt. If he could not gain control of Pantone Press, he would leave and start his own business.

No surprise registered on Jesse Levine's face. His calm demeanor spoke of relief as he stated he would check with his brother Mervyn to "see what was going on." Larry felt in his gut that they would take the deal.

The buyout, to the tune of the full $50,000, was finalized less than a week later in the beginning of May 1962. Larry insisted that the purchase amount be plowed back into the company to enhance the balance sheets, rather than into the brothers' pockets. In return for complete control, Larry would take over their debt. Unencumbered, the Levine brothers were free to return to their erstwhile advertising agency business, Jesse and Mervyn Levine Advertising.

The purchase of Pantone would prove to be a steal for Larry, who would wind up carving out an empire from a perception — something he couldn't even own.

THE KING *of* COLOR

2

The Man Behind the Rainbow

Larry never planned to make a career in the print industry. It simply existed in the background, unnoticed, like buttons or zippers that magically appeared and aided us in our daily lives. By age twelve, however, the innate talent that would generate a whole new industry had become evident. In 1941, as a middle-grader in Arthur Somers Intermediate School in Brooklyn, Larry took the requisite shop classes that prepared young men in trades like electrical wiring, woodworking, sheet metal and printing. The print shop, a cool, innocuous gray room positioned at a corridor's end, turned into Larry's haven. There, he explored the intricacies and nature of ink.

As did most school children, Larry already understood the basics of color from mixing finger and poster paints — the primaries: red, yellow and blue and, from them, the secondary colors: orange, green and purple. Ink's consistency was different though. To ensure a satisfactory print each time on the shop's platen press, applications to the rollers required constant attention. Any irregular consistency

JUST TH-INK

Though the first U.S. commercial ink factory was founded in 1742, the Chinese had developed an ink substance used in negative relief printing of pictures and text from stone surfaces over 5000 years prior. The substance from which inks were made and used for centuries to come was soot mixed with glue rendered from animal skins.

As ink continued to evolve, it became clear that writing inks could not adhere to printing surfaces of paper without bleeding through. At one point, around the time of German inventor Johannes Gutenberg in 1450, painter Jan van Eyck experimented with boiling artists paints, which were based in oil, to create a thicker substance. Gutenberg's oil-based inks had been formulated from van Eyck's work.

in the ink meant an uneven application and inferior print results, so a self-assured Larry took it upon himself to supervise.

While the print shop was the source of the school's publishing program, this challenge was more than purely academic and right up Larry's alley. Larry not only enjoyed printing, he excelled at it. He could hand-set type, selecting the individual letters and placing them on a composing stick to form words and sentences, run the platen press and pull proofs more quickly than anyone. More importantly, though, he understood how the press worked.

The twelve-year-old often tinkered with the antiquated press while cleaning and maintaining it. Though it only handled one color at a time, Larry mastered the machine and commanded the inks to respond. Always offering up a single color as the platen moved up and around to receive an even distribution of ink and down to print the image, copies soared from the press as quickly as Larry's hands could move. In the process, he churned out simple black and white school announcements and newsletters. As color paper was considered a commodity, and the dispirited times did not warrant excessive spending, the invitations and official school stationery he also created were generally in ecru — a word derived from the French meaning "unbleached" — and equally insipid.

Recognizing the youngster's gift and aware of how helpful Larry could be, the print shop teacher managed to enroll Larry permanently in a class that he otherwise would have attended for a single term. For Larry, the experience inspired approval he didn't often freely receive from his hardworking immigrant parents, especially his father, Harry Herbert. Harry had held a position as a movie projectionist since Larry was five years old. Though it offered more stability than the temporary Depression Era carpentry jobs for which he endured long lines and even longer hours to receive $3 a day, the odd shifts in Manhattan theaters and later, in the Bronx, meant precious little family time. So, Harry was rarely around to share in his son's accomplishments. Though his mother remained at home, she kept busy with the house and cooking. As a result, Larry sought solace in his school projects.

Larry took on the task of learning with vigor, even playfulness. When presented with his first typesetting assignment early in that school year, he paraphrased the famous line by playwright George Farquhar (1678-1707), 'Necessity is the mother of invention.' The choice of phrase would prove prophetic.

Secure in his abilities before the end of the school year, Larry began to experiment with the press. Challenging the status quo, which was rarely good enough for Larry, prompted him to try to print three colors at one time on the solitary color press. First, he carved an oak leaf into a linoleum block and placed it on the press. For Larry, this sole leaf represented the multitude of leaves that changed colors each fall in Brooklyn's Prospect Park, where he and friends often played. Next, he inked the roller in green, yellow and red bands, then disconnected the device that turned the platen. Finally, he began to print the leaf image.

The result was less than pleasing. Something had gone wrong. The trio of colors stiffened and refused to blend.

Larry didn't allow the problematic inexpensive inks to defeat him. Instead, he thinned the inks' consistency by adding linseed oil. This time, his autumn leaf print rolled out from the press in final soft tones of green to yellow-green, yellow to orange and finally red. Larry's teacher, impressed with his student's tenaciousness and ingenuity, submitted the fall leaf experiment for a National Graphics Award. Larry won.

SOMBER REFLECTIONS

An era disadvantaged in numerous ways, the '30s sported grays, maroons and similarly morose shades, colors which not only reflected the times, but the tough economy. The textile dye industry during that time stretched expensive colors by diluting them with black. By decade's end, color re-emerged as a sign of renewal. With the onset of World War II and the shortage of goods once again, color remained one of life's few respites.

Even as a young child, Larry had shown an affinity for color, much to his mother's delight. After Harry Herbert's once thriving business, Herbert Cabinetry and Supplies, failed before the onset of the Depression, the Herberts — Harry, Elsie, and sister Billie (Beulah) — relocated from fashionable Bensonhurst to the immigrant neighborhood of Brownsville/Flatbush in Brooklyn where Larry was soon born. Elsie Herbert maintained their cramped quarters in the tiny fourth floor walk-up at 351 Legion Street with plenty of verve and very little money. Each day she arose and put on one of two housecoats: pale pink and deep rose colored floral, or pale butter yellow with greenery. The apartment's main room, which functioned as both a dining and living area, served as the family gathering place to talk, read or be entertained by the popular 1930s radio shows of

COMING UP ROSES

While the Democrats launched their 1932 presidential
campaign promising that 'Everything will be Rosy with
Roosevelt,'[8] the association of the color rose with things
positive was not new. The expression "rose-colored glasses"
goes back to at least 1861, when it is first recorded in
Tom Brown at Oxford: "Oxford was a sort of Utopia to
the Captain. He continued to behold towers, and quad-
rangles, and chapels, through rose-colored glasses."[9]

comedy team Amos and Andy, songstress Kate Smith, Major Bowes
Amateur Hour, and later, by FDR's Fireside Chats on their dark
wood, cathedral-shaped tabletop RCA. Larry even came home for
lunch during school and listened to the O'Neals with his mother.
Though the family of four remained in the tiny Single bedroom
apartment for some time, Elsie managed to add cheer with gutsy,
vibrantly-colored fabrics in yellow, green and blue she saved from the
'20s Jazz Age, and an equally bright attitude. Still too young to be
aware of the grim economic climate of the Depression and shielded
from his parents' difficulties, young Larry delighted in helping his
mother set the dining table, which she managed to turn into a game.

---

[8] *"Random House Dictionary of Popular Proverbs and Sayings" by Gregory Y. Titelman (Random House, New York,1996).*
[9] *"Encyclopedia of Word and Phrase Origins" by Robert Hendrickson (Facts on File, New York, 1997)*

She described each item by color as she lovingly directed her son to assist.

Color shifts and trends during the early twentieth century went generally unnoticed by most. The wealthy patrons of fashion designers and Hollywood's finest fancied trendy colors, but the masses lived with palettes somewhat more abbreviated — until, that is, the postwar 1950s shook everything up.

"First we spread the pink and lavender flower bordered table-cloth on the table," she began.

Next came the rose patterned dinnerware acquired from attending Tuesday night movie serials at the Ambassador Theater on Saratoga Avenue. (After paying her nickel and collecting her ornate, floral-patterned dish, Elsie would often pass up the actual show.) Snowy white napkins, which were generally tucked away after dinner and reused throughout the week, followed by simply-styled, initialed silverware purchased from Kellogg's Corn Flakes with cereal box tops and, finally, the incongruous clear Yahrzeit can dle[10] drinking glasses completed the table setting. According to Elsie, at the end of the day, having the family gathered at the heavily-adorned, dark, thick wooden dinner table made everything feel right, even rosy.

Too soon, though, Elsie would have to give up the last vestige that reminded her of the more genteel life she had once known in her

---

[10] *Wax and a wick inside what appears to be a clear drinking glass and customarily lit each year on the date of passing of a family member and on certain festivals in that person's memory.*

homeland of England — her handsome mahogany dining set. With older daughter Billie and young Larry growing, the ten-by-ten-foot bedroom could no longer accommodate the foursome. The Herberts traded Elsie's dining set for a 'pull-out' sofa where she and Harry would sleep, while Billie and Larry remained in the bedroom in their single beds. Elsie took little consolation in the fact that the living room set was "fashionably" upholstered in a striped maroon (from the French word for the reddish-brown chestnut) and gray. She referred to the fabric as 'dingy red' and 'not so black,' colors she thought drab and sorrowful. The effect was worsened by the solid maroon sitting chair which even to Larry's young eye appeared a different color from the rest and didn't quite match. All this contrasted pitifully with Elsie's favorite colors, rosy pink, sunshine yellow and springtime green, all so clear, bright and cheerful.

During those Depression years, the macadam streets, wooden and brick structures of the surrounding neighborhood buildings remained dulled even under the most brilliant summer sunshine, and all but disappeared into the steely winter sky. Even red brick remained mute. A lower income area that spawned shopkeepers, tradespeople and factory workers, most of these immigrants' lives mirrored the neighborhood's drabness.

The country emerged from the Depression only to plunge into war. Citizens were once again requested to tighten their belts, this time for the war effort. The Herbert family's belts, however, had already been cinched for years. Though Elsie budgeted money from

Harry's occasional private carpentry jobs and President Roosevelt's Home Relief program, she had to employ her shopping prowess to keep the family well fed. Elsie shunned the more expensive stores on Pitkin Avenue and the small grocery that stood nearby the house, and instead shopped the pushcarts that came by where she bought fresh vegetables and live fish. Weekly, she walked twenty blocks round-trip to Belmont Avenue through an even more marginal neighborhood to negotiate bargains for the table. Each weekly trip filled two shopping bundles that the small, slender woman carried extended from each arm. Elsie created her meals with the care and adeptness learned from her own mother of nine children to provide daily sustenance before her next shopping trip.

As Larry's world began to expand beyond the walls of home, he remained unaware of his parents' struggles or that they, like others, had been on Home Relief. Elsie and Harry protected their children as best they could from outward strife, as well as from a neighborhood that saw occasional shootings and only had a pool hall and movie theatre for local entertainment. Larry's favorite movie, *The Charge of the Light Brigade* (1936), featured the suave and bold Errol Flynn who always saved the day. Like his hero, Larry would learn to be tough and resourceful. And he would do it on his own.

Always a polite and quiet child in school, the award of a merit star by his first grade teacher, Miss Patterson, proved an open invitation for other students to pick on him. To worsen matters, he began to sport a British accent mimicking Aunt Lea, his mother's older sister, who lived with the Herberts for six months after arriving from England. This feigned display brought jeers and more than one throttling. But, when a rock was thrown at his head during a playground incident, causing blood to trickle over his face and on to his freshly laundered white shirt and brown knickers, Larry vowed never to let the bigger guys get to him again. The next playground confrontation ended with the bully crying and running away. He would internalize this lesson and carry it with him the rest of his life. The Herberts' financial woes eased after Larry's father applied for work as a moving picture operator. The much sought-after job, though, nearly vanished as quickly as it had materialized. Securing the position required Harry to join the projectionists' union at a cost to him of $2,000 — a sum grand enough to buy a house at the time. Harry got lucky. As no one could afford such an amount, and the union needed projectionists, they allowed individuals to take the positions and pay off the debt over a four-year period. Harry became a theater projectionist on Broadway in Manhattan, giving him a somewhat plumper paycheck than he would have earned in a local neighborhood theater. His steady paycheck as a motion picture operator, along with the occasional side job he took off-the-books as a cabinetmaker, gave the family some financial leeway, and they moved to larger quarters.

The Cape Cod-style home they rented a few blocks away on East 59th Street between Church and Snyder Streets, complete with yard and coop for the pigeons Larry had befriended on the fire escape of their tiny rear-facing apartment, would remain their home for his middle school years. Fire escapes, an integral part of pre-turn-of-the-century immigrant tenement buildings, were used for everything but what they were intended. Oftentimes, they added extra storage for bicycles and such. In cooler weather, potatoes, onions, even butter, could be stored in a bin outside. In the heights of the summer, they served as a respite and a place from which neighbors could converse. For Larry, it became a place to harbor 'pets.' He and his father built a pigeon coop from a crate and hung it from the fire escape where Larry could feed and care for the birds. Larry had even fashioned a shade to offer the birds privacy and protection from the elements. When the family moved to East New York, a chicken coop became the pigeons' home, until Larry left the coop door open one day and the birds returned to their old address.

Hoping that the darkest days were behind them now, the Herberts looked forward to their son's upcoming Bar Mitzvah in January 1942. Young Larry had studied diligently the past two years to make his parents proud, learning the Torah in Hebrew and his speech in Yiddish. Never dissuaded by a challenge, Larry scheduled his schoolwork, Hebrew studies and Boy Scout meetings, with executive flair. He was determined to make his parents proud as he stood in front of the synagogue's congregation. But life had its way of throwing curves.

On Sunday morning, December 7, 1941, the family thought about an outing. The weather had been extremely mild the past few weeks, and the Herberts decided to take advantage of the extended fall-like season to visit Aunt Lea in the Bronx. This morning, though, the weather suddenly turned raw and bitter. They changed their plans and decided to stay home. As Elsie cleared the breakfast table, Harry turned on the radio to the shocking news that the Japanese had bombed Pearl Harbor. Whether due to the frigid air or the crushing news of war — or both — nobody strode the streets of Brooklyn that day. Uncertain of what the immediate future would bring, Larry's Bar Mitzvah, planned around his thirteenth birthday in January, was postponed.

The big event finally took place on a warm, sunny, spring-like day in March, with the proceedings held in a room at the nearby Mohilev Old Age Home on Snyder Avenue. As a member of the Ladies Auxiliary that volunteered there, Elsie had managed to procure the space. More importantly, the sparse, unadorned Home owned a Torah from which Larry could read his Bar Mitzvah passages. The family gathered: Elsie donned her navy blue going-to-Shul dress and hat with a purplish-pink flower cluster, Harry, a dark suit and hat, Billie, a floral dress, and Larry, a new single-breasted tan worsted. He recited his Bar Mitzvah speech in Yiddish. It began "Meine teiere eltern…My dear parents and my dear family, today is a very special day for me." Rite of passage completed, the group returned to the Herbert household for a sumptuous spread prepared by Elsie, including chopped liver, egg salad, gefilte fish and herring, as Larry received the traditional gift envelopes of money. Later, as Elsie cleaned up, Larry opened his presents and counted: $60 and a black pen. Compared to the lavish multi-media Hollywood-theme festivity attended by hundreds with which he would regale his second son, Loren, some fifty years later, this solemn occasion began a new chapter in Larry's life.

Though he had worked hard to prepare for this day, he realized for the first time that his parents had too. Certain that the Bar Mitzvah cost them dearly, he handed the money to his mother. Until that day, he hadn't understood the significance of contributing to his family or having his own money. Soon after, though, he took an after-school job at a local fruit store delivering orders for fifteen cents an hour plus tips. Larry had become a man.

The shortage of money that Larry had known throughout his childhood persisted. He understood and respected his father's talent as a cabinetmaker but realized all too quickly that his father lacked any business acumen. Jobs that Harry secured during the Depression and beyond came only after standing in long lines and working even longer hours. A good-natured, uncomplaining man, his occasional private clients readily took advantage of his situation. Larry had even stood witness to his father's unfair treatment during the remodeling of a doctor's home. Harry had come highly recommended. He could do anything when it came to construction. And, on this particular job, the doctor agreed to pay in cash. When the job neared completion, the doctor complained that Harry hadn't done the work properly and released him without pay. When Larry's father did not take a stand in his own defense, the outraged and broken-hearted youngster approached the doctor's wife on his father's behalf. Larry had helped on this particular job, so he knew nothing had gone wrong with the work. Even so, Larry, himself handy, offered to fix any problems the couple could point out. They identified none and still refused to pay. As much as he felt for his father, Larry soon came to realize that his father would always struggle to make enough money. That was something Larry was determined never to do.

3

Growing Up in the Printing Industry

At 16, still restless and hungry for funds, Larry took a job at Schulte Press in Manhattan. He would occupy the position of a 'printer's devil' — a lackey who cleaned the presses and put away type — a post that had belonged to a seventeen-year-old friend leaving for the Navy. The two spent sufficient time together for Larry to not only acquaint himself with, but master, the various presses. The future called, but Larry couldn't hear it over the din of printing presses. His lowly position only reminded him of what he didn't have.

There had to be a better way, he thought. Clarity came most unexpectedly one day on an outing with his dad. The rare, but prized, father-son time was often spent fishing in Jamaica Bay. On a warm, pre-summer day, as the sun bobbed and sank in the water, the two trailed their rods off the pier. Larry looked at the spit of land across the Bay and the small drifting powerboats practically within reach. As flashes of white and blue sped past them, he turned to his father and asked why they didn't have their own boat like everyone else.

"Well, Mr. Fancy Pants, who has money to buy a boat? What do you think, I'm a rich doctor?" replied Harry.

Suddenly, sixteen-year-old Larry had his answer: he would become a rich, respected doctor and never worry about money again.

Medical school would take money his parents did not have, so Larry kept his job at Schulte Press throughout high school and began to save with that goal in mind. Knowing that college would be right around the corner, he also took his studies more seriously, excelling as a result in biology, chemistry and physics. After graduating high school in January 1947, he immediately began classes at Brooklyn College, scheduling his shifts at Schulte Press around his classes. Occasionally, he even gave up sleep in order to take the odd midnight shift at other printing plants for extra cash.

Even though the fashion color palettes had shifted from the less somber tones of the '30s to those reflective of patriotism, printing work during World War II remained mundane. Basically, Schulte printed jobs for Grace Church next door. "It was pretty much a black, white and gray world," recalls Larry. "The building was gray. The ink was black and the paper white." The companies Larry moonlighted for, however, gave the late teen his first taste of working with color. He produced labels for medications, which may have indirectly been part of the war effort, as well as medical journals, a catalog for a liquor company, and a trade publication called *Business International.* His key achievement occurred when he began to print a journal called *Production Wise.* This industry bible on all-things-production always came adorned with a full-color cover, which Larry worked on.

Though he was unaware of it at the time, the job would launch Larry's full-time education on color, an education that would last a lifetime. Color had always been a fact of life, but not necessarily in printing, and especially not during the war when everything was scarce. Printers undertook any job, and with budgets tightened, requests mainly came for black and white. As the post-war economy geared up, advertisers and publishers imagined new possibilities. *Seventeen* magazine debuted along with a growing teen marketing trend. Women's fashion returned from minimalist Rosie the Riveter dreary to sweeping, feminine and romantic with soft sheer colors to match. When no one else would take on color printing jobs, they were handed to Larry, who savored the experience to learn.

Larry's well-planned routine evaporated when the job at Schulte ended. The owners sold the business and the new operators replaced the familiar equipment with updated, more complicated models. Larry could have learned to run the new equipment — his talent and intelligence had proved that. He also realized that no matter how proficient he was at printing, being a pressman for the rest of his life would be the death of his dream. If he wanted to go to medical school, he had to concentrate on his premed studies at a college reputed in preparing students for medical school.

The following semester he transferred to Long Island's Hofstra College and began night courses while working during the day at Stuyvesant Press — his new employer. Then he switched to day courses and worked at night, eventually earning more money than his father. Either way, the atmosphere at Hofstra energized Larry and gave him a taste of the good life. He joined a fraternity and socialized with upper middle class students, as well as World War II army veterans making use of the GI Bill. Though he saved most of the disposable income from his job for college, he was still able to buy his first car, a two-toned 1950 Pontiac Catalina, with a rust-colored hard top, a cream-colored body, and a rust and cream interior. With car colors moving into the realm of softer pastels, such as blues and greens, as well as two-tone looks, Larry's car exemplified the perfect transition from one era to the next. It both fit in and stood out. The mechanically adept young man now drove both a piece of art and a great pick-up car.

At last he felt that he belonged. And he felt comfortable in his determination. He would pursue a career in medicine and reap the rewards. Ironically, Larry would wind up making his home — and his mark — not in medicine but rather in the industry originally intended simply to finance that dream.

In 1951, Larry graduated Hofstra with a bachelor's degree in biology and chemistry, but not without incident. Just four days prior to commencement, he and a friend set out on a motorcycle excursion with Larry straddling the back. Not far from home, they careened into a car that had run a red light driven by a young, unlicensed boy who had 'borrowed' his mother's car. Larry flew over the vehicle,

1951 Medical school application photo

landed on his shoulder and skid along the pavement, lacerating his leg and head.

Reassuring his family he would be well enough to attend commencement ceremonies, he was released from Kings County Hospital that same day, his wavy brown hair bandaged in white. The first in the entire family to attend and graduate college, he was not about to miss this auspicious occasion. Calling upon his "never say never" attitude and "Mother Necessity" once again, Larry enlisted the aid of his two closest fraternity brothers.

"Look, I have trouble walking and I've got this bandage on my head and I know we aren't wearing caps. How the hell am I going to get through this?" he asked.

"We'll figure something out. Let us take care of it. Just show up," responded his fraternity brother.

On the day of graduation with his parents, aunts and uncles looking on, his buddies disguised his white head bandage as best they could with black electrician tape. Knowing that they would be called in groups of three, they repositioned him to an aisle seat. When the threesome that included Larry was called, his buddies scooped him up, one on either side, and marched him to the stage to receive his diploma.

Eager to attend medical school upon graduation, Larry discovered a new set of challenges. For every position available, thousands had applied. World War II veterans who had finally made it into college in 1946 and 1947 graduated at the same time as Larry, and, under the GI Bill, many applied to medical school as well. Further, the unspoken quota against Jewish applicants to medical schools, in place since the 1920s, became even more restrictive.[11] With this onrush of applicants, Larry was keenly advised not to apply: the odds were stacked too strongly against him.

Still determined, though in need of more money to pay for costly tuition, books, room and board, Larry decided on a new course of action. Deciding that he, too, would put the GI Bill to work for him, he volunteered for the Korean War draft. He was inducted and sent to Korea with the distinguished 3rd Infantry Division in October 1951. He had remembered his father's stories of World War I. As a young man and one of fifteen children of an immigrant Russian family in London, Harry Herbert (previously known as Israel Hubbersgilt) joined the Royal Air Force as an aircraft gunner. Shot down over Belgium, he remained hospitalized for several months overseas.

After nearly two harrowing years spent in a foxhole and as a non-commissioned officer in charge of operational intelligence in the combat zone, Larry returned home on July 27, 1953, the day the Armistice was signed. Life back home during Larry's absence had moved at a breakneck pace. While he lived in tents and foxholes in Korea, suburban cookie-cutter neighborhoods and towns cropped up

---

[11] *Belth, Nathan, A Promise To Keep: A Narrative of the American Encounter with Anti-Semitism, 1979 Times Books (also listed as Crown Publishers), New York. Also lists 1981 Schocken Books.*

1952 Chunchon Korea

like weeds. Builders like Levitt and designers like Eichler crafted affordable tract homes for boomer families on both coasts. Consumers brandished the dollar and caught the attention of manufacturers, who now spent over 36 percent of their advertising dollars in newspapers and as little as 3 percent for TV, despite the fact that some 93 percent of households owned a TV set.

Larry tried to pick up where he left off, but the changes proved overwhelming. The flashy new bright red Corvette now chased down the highways while chasing 'reds' had become Senator McCarthy's favorite sport. Reassuringly, the sporting Yankees had won two more World series in a row, and the Bible had outsold all other books for a second year in a row. Though Ethel and Julius Rosenberg had been put to death, Ian Fleming's James Bond had been born, Saran wrapped our food in plastic, fish squared off into a stick, our Cheez Whiz-zed from a can and Swanson gave us another reason to sit in front of the TV — dinner in aluminum trays. Though gas and milk had both risen $.02, at least postage stamps remained steady at $.03.

Feeling somewhat less than a hero of the Forgotten War, and alien to the classroom atmosphere, Larry approached his medical school mission cautiously. To reacquaint himself with the task of studying, he took graduate school courses at Hofstra and NYU.

To add to his quandary, he had moved back to his parents' home in Brooklyn, a constant reminder of lesser things. The home he had left behind now looked pathetically small after living in open spaces.

THE KING *of* COLOR

OFFSET PRINTING PRIMER

*In offset printing, an offshoot of the original stone
lithography fashioned in 1796 by playwright Alois
Senefelder of Munich to reproduce his plays, water
rollers dampen the image plate to reject ink on non-
image areas. The ink tray (or fountain) evenly releases
ink onto the image cylinder (lithoplate), where it then
adheres to the image area only. The image is transferred
to a rubber blanket cylinder (known as offset) then
printed to the paper. This process facilitated the printing
of newer pastel colors, which were becoming increasingly
popular, and which had proved increasingly difficult to
print using the letterpress, thick ink, direct print method.*

His mother, too, appeared somehow diminished. Most of his friends
were gone — married with families of their own. His only link to the
static old neighborhood remained the girl across the street, Roberta,
who had corresponded with him during the war. Her letters had been
comforting and enthusiastic, and now that he was home, he courted
the young hat model. They married a year later and moved to a
studio apartment in Queens, just outside Manhattan.

Settled in their cozy space — furnished with a newly acquired
black sleeper sofa, turquoise and pink side chairs, and a black
Formica-topped dinette set with gray seat cushions — and comfort-

able with his academic abilities, Larry applied to medical schools. While awaiting replies, he resumed his position at Stuyvesant Press, 445 Pearl Street in Manhattan. Though he'd worked at the company for only a short stint (at $96 a week) before entering the army, Larry had made an impression. Stuyvesant Press had launched Larry's education in color printing and matching with the full-color covers for the trade magazine *Production Wise*. Owner Al Manette had been so impressed with Larry's aptitude during that period that during the war years, he had called Larry's mom every three months to check in. "Is he home yet?" he'd ask eagerly. "When is he due home?"

The Korean Conflict had not affected the burgeoning home economy. Independent, family-owned printers would increase to 89,000 in the United States alone within the next decade, making the printing industry the second largest employer in the U.S. Accordingly, Manette welcomed the hard-working and intelligent young man back as a pressman and apprentice color matcher, a newly-created role, and offered him $125 a week.

Larry learned the art of commercial color matching on the job. Stuyvesant maintained their color inks in cans. So when a client asked for red, it usually came straight out of that single can of red. If a customer proclaimed he didn't like the red, that it was too dull and needed livening, Larry would incrementally add yellow to brighten it. Eventually the job took on dimension. Color requests of all types came from the clients wanting a little more this, a little less that, a little softer, etc. Larry quickly became a blending master, spending

41

TYPESETTING

*Until the 1950s, the majority of typesetting was
Performed mechanically with a Linotype machine,
which produced a "slug" or line of type from hot metal,
generally referred to as "hot type." Further, maintaining
line height consistency from one line to the next became
an issue with mechanical type formulating, something
Larry forestalled by requiring a special measuring device.
Typesetting (photo image composition), the method
used with the introduction of commercial offset printing
in the early 1950s, made use of a photographic image of
the type to create a printing plate.*

hours at the ink-mixing table perfecting colors to ensure that clients got exactly what they wanted.

His feel for ink, which he had displayed at such a young age, never betrayed him. At one point, the owner of Printing Impression's magazine, *Printing Wise,* wanted to show a sunset on the cover of the magazine. When the two separate plates ran on the letterpress, laying down the lighter top area for the sunset, then the lower dark area for the horizon, the resulting image turned murky. Larry offered a solution. "We need a little more blue at the bottom plate and more orange at the top plate." When they ran the cover again, blending colors from one plate over the other, a dramatic sunset emerged.

Larry quickly proved his value as a pressman as well. At the end of a particularly busy day, when he was due to take his new wife to dinner, he was called upon to run a rush job, a special report for Business International printed black on light green paper. Determined not to be late for the previously planned evening, he geared up. The pre-press operations, typesetting, color separation, and image carrier preparation had been completed and awaited him. First, he requested his reserve of quick-drying inks. He set up two presses and ran them at a dizzying speed of 5,000 sheets per hour, finishing the job of 15,000 impressions from two forms in one hour and 40 minutes. While the second press ran, he washed and dressed. He then did the unthinkable. To postpone his clean-up until the next day, Larry poured machine oil (as opposed to linseed oil, which contains a drying agent) onto the ink rollers. Though not standard procedure after a press run, Larry knew from his experiences over the years that this method would keep the ink from drying. He recognized that leaving the oiled rollers wouldn't present a problem. In the old days, the pressman had even been known to use Vaseline.

Larry had, in fact, told his boss of his plan. He offered him a choice. "Look, Al, I can stay here another half hour, washing this press at overtime rates," he chuckled. "Or I can clean it the first thing in the morning at the basic rates." His boss chose the latter.

The press foreman disagreed with Larry's approach. Responsible for the presses and press time, he came down hard on Larry the next morning and complained about the additional work Larry had created for everyone by delaying the clean-up. But co-owner Al Manette saw it differently.

Prompted by frequent chats about the future of the printing business during their long subway rides together to Queens, Manette viewed Larry as a forward thinker. Larry displayed a knowledge and enthusiasm for the latest technological changes in printing and even boldly recommended that Stuyvesant replace their presses with the newer, highly touted offset printing techniques (both sheetfed and web, or continuous roll), a lithographic method of printing using the underlying principle that ink and water do not mix.

Though offset printing would see its phenomenal growth in the U.S. in the early 1960s, producing the nation's magazines and news-papers by 1962, it had been around since 1905. Still, printers were slow to embrace offset. The investment expense alone for new equipment prohibited many small and medium size printers from switching, so they remained loyal to letterpress, a printing system dating back to 700 A.D. China and using raised type or images.

Though unhurried to institute Larry's recommendation, Manette elevated Larry to the position as foreman at Stuyvesant. At the same time, Larry was inducted the youngest union pressman in New York at that time, which helped raise his pay. These accomplishments in just over two short years, which brought Larry both pay and position increases, also created internal jealousies. As foreman, Larry essentially ran the pressroom. Manette's business partner, Irving Levinson, became increasingly agitated by Larry's having Manette's ear, especially when Larry recommended scuttling traditional letter-press for offset printing in writing. Larry's proposal to the two men included a complete rationale for the addition of offset equipment. While Manette handled sales operations, Levinson's charge was the press's composing room, a duty solidly threatened with obsolescence by Larry's suggestion.

The partners had known each other since their days in the army, and when Levinson insisted on replacing Larry as foreman, Al knew that the proud and headstrong innovator would not take a step back. With a heavy heart, he recommended that Larry leave Stuyvesant Press and secure a position elsewhere.

Still doggedly determined to attend medical school, Larry needed more money for tuition. He immediately initiated a search for a new job. That same month, June 1956, he strolled into the 22-story Printing Crafts Building which ran the full block between 33rd and 34th Streets on the west side of Eighth Avenue in Manhattan. Skirted by the General Post Office and Pennsylvania Station, where Madison Square Garden now stands, and just two blocks from Macy's department store, the elegant 1916 building (now called 5 Penn Plaza), at the time supposedly the largest in the country devoted to publishing and printing, was ideally located as the uptown center of the printing trades. Embellished Corinthian columns and sculpted gold filigree adorning the building's exterior masked the substantial load-bearing floors meant to accommodate the massive presses that churned twenty-four hours a day.

COLOR ATTRIBUTES

There are literally millions of colors! Fortunately, they can be divided into just a few color families. And every color can be described in terms of having three main attributes: hue, saturation and brightness.

Hue, directly linked to the color's wavelength, is identified as the color family or color name (such as red, green, purple).

Saturation, also called "chroma," is a measure of the purity of a color or how sharp or dull the color appears.

Brightness, also called "luminance" or "value," is the shade (darkness) or tint (lightness) of a color. Areas of an evenly-colored object in direct light have higher brightness than areas in shadow.[12]

Larry walked into the offices of Pantone Press. With his flair for color and several years' printing experience, he applied for a position as a precision color matcher, a job he heard about through an employment agency that had placed him on jobs while he was in school. The unoccupied position had belonged to a pressman, who, with one of Pantone's salesmen, had ventured out on his own. Larry applied to run the pressroom to assume duties as color matcher. After an extensive interview and a commendation from Stuyvesant regarding his skill as

[12] *Pantone, Inc., Color Think Tank.*
   http://www.pantone.com/products/products.aspfiidArticle=110&idArea=16

"an expert color matcher," the head of production at Pantone recommended Larry for the position. The Levine brothers, who owned Pantone, concurred but offered him the low salary of $125 a week.

"That's unacceptable," said Larry. "I make $140 now. (Although he wrote on his application form that he made $ 165 as foreman when he left Stuyvesant, Larry worked a significant amount of overtime since his base salary was recorded as $140 for a forty-hour work week.) I know presses. And I know color matching."

The Levines upped their offer to $130 a week. Larry took the job knowing he would be leaving for the University of Alabama Medical School in just three months.

THE KING *of* COLOR

4

Finding a Calling and a Home

"I'm pregnant," Larry's wife informed him a few short weeks before his departure for medical school. Feeling a new sense of responsibility, somewhat tired after waiting nearly two years to be accepted into medical school, as well as a little too old to be a student, Larry focused on a new future: his family and, unbeknownst to him, Pantone. In his wildest dreams, he would not have predicted that in less than ten years, he would turn Pantone — a small, unknown company — into a monolith.

During his probationary period at Pantone, Larry had proved his worth to the company. He had replaced two men: the color matcher, who had left to form a competitive company, and the salesman who had defected with him. As September — Larry's anticipated medical school start date — rolled near, the Levine brothers asked Larry to stay. Consumerism had proven a strong providence, product display printing had increased as everyone's focus had turned to color.

To sweeten the pot, they offered Larry a salary increase of $10, raising his weekly pay from $130 to $140. Realizing just how far he'd come and how fast, Larry began questioning his motives behind medical school. Did he really want to be a doctor at age twenty-seven? How would he support his family?

Like the Sirens' call, the hum of the presses sang to him as (and) the perfume of ink enticed him to stay.

Having made the decision to keep his job, Larry dove in to fix Pantone's immediate problem — the custom color cards Pantone had produced for years, used by cosmetic companies for point-of-purchase displays, faded too rapidly. With increasing requests for additional pastel colors and variations of pinks and reds for the cosmetic palettes, Larry began by overhauling the pigment selections, then turned his thoughts to modifying the machinery.

Letterpress printing, the most widely used commercial printing method of the time, printed images by laying down a thick coat of ink from a roller to an etched image plate, which was then directly imprinted onto the paper. Logically, denser ink layering should have meant a longer product shelf-life with less overall fading. But inks were mixed by hand and every batch varied. Pigments of powder or granules were blended with varnishes, oils and drying substances.[13] As pigment has no drying properties of its own, the tiniest amount added to a mix boosted its drying capacity. If the selected pigments were not suspended properly — encapsulated into the liquid agent

---

[13] *These included manganese and cobalt — unusual substances, as they are often considered colorants themselves.*

— the ink's impurities, or residual grind, came through on the final product as flaws. Overall, these coarse suspensions offered less color intensity than the subsequent inks that came with the offset method of printing. As a consequence, they faded more rapidly.

To prevent display cards for Max Factor's hot pink lipstick or Revlon's cherry red nail polish from turning pale baby pink, or Clairol's golden blond locks from turning ashen, Larry revamped the inks. As 100 percent fade-proof inks did not (and still do not) exist, Larry sought to make them as fade-resistant as possible. Tougher, 100 percent light resistant Rubine red pigment replaced the more fragile magenta-like Rhodamine red pigment. Densely pigmented chrome yellow (lead chromate pigment was first extracted from the rare mineral crocoite by the French pharmacist and chemist Louis Vauquelin in 1809), though not used today because of its lead content, was a staple for letterpress work.

The working presses at Pantone, in constant use since 1946, came next on Larry's 'to do' list. During his first several months at Pantone, Larry had discussed his idea of a high-volume split fountain press with owner Jesse Levine, and finally received a green light to produce it. Inventiveness came naturally to Larry. Handling internal conflict and petty jealousies did not.

At Stuyvesant Press, Larry had contended with both. Pantone would usher in his first taste of active betrayal and industry politics. He spent the next twelve months experimenting with inks and developing the split fountain printing equipment, a bit of genius

AS THE WHEEL TURNS

The concept of the color wheel was invented when
Sir Isaac Newton bent the color spectrum into a circle.
Since then, the color wheel has been used as a tool
for understanding color relationships and creating
harmonious color schemes. The color wheel clearly
shows which colors are warm and cool, complementary,
split complementary and analogous.[14]

which would eventually not only give him the edge on other printers, but would also lead to the method by which he would manufacture his first 50,000 PANTONE MATCHING SYSTEM Color books. He remembered the little platen press he had worked on in middle school: the roller rose to catch the ink released from the channel and fell onto the form for printing. This first experiment had lead to others, including one while at Stuyvesant Press in the early 1950s.

Occasionally a printing job came along that required an odd-sized paper. To use the entire width of the ink fountain meant wasting ink and precious time cleaning up. Larry had the idea to reduce the fountain to match the width of the paper. He accomplished this by damming the outsides of the fountain. This precursor form of

[14] *Pantone, Inc., Color Think Tank*
 http://www.pantone.com/products/products.aspfiidArticle=110&idArea=16

fountain splitting allowed only the center portion of the fountain to hold and release ink. This, he determined, would be the basis for his design as he directed the two machinists he hired from within the building.

"Build this machine like you are building a precision watch," he told them and pressed on. "I want the clearance to be very, very snug — just enough so it can go up and down, releasing the ink, and tight enough so it won't have any leaks."

Accuracy, and not pressure, was key to controlling the flow of ink and not damaging the ink roller. Since twenty-one keys regulated the ink flow from the fountain, he carefully calculated proportions and split the fountain into twenty-one separate sections. His first step, almost school-like in approach, required no more than cardboard, duct tape and scissors. Each piece of cardboard, fitted and taped between the keys in the fountain, became a dam for a new color trough.

Larry continued the process until he found materials tough enough to withstand extensive print runs. Then the machinists took over. Precision-tooled metal dividers performed the best. Fired up after nearly a year of trial and error, Larry and one of the Pantone pressmen readied the press for its premiere run.

"It'll never work," asserted the pressman who had helped him set up the press and fountains.

"Explain why not," asked Larry impatiently.

As Larry pushed for an explanation, the pressman said he would show him what was wrong. Before Larry could stop him, he turned a middle key, which tightened the steel fountain blade against the ink roller and damaged it. Larry stood by stunned. This senseless act would set him back.

Anger and frustration rushed in.

"What the hell are you doing?" Larry squawked.

He knew that any pressman worth his salt understood the step-down sequence of key adjustments. Had the project been sabotaged because the pressman felt his job in jeopardy? Was there some conspiracy against Larry?

Whichever the case, Larry would not be dissuaded and started over. Over the next couple of weeks, the man who neighbors had said could fix anything retooled the damaged roller, then set up the press himself. He alone would test the integrity of the machine for leaks or crossover color. Alternating yellow and dark blue, the fountain troughs were filled with a mere sliver preventing them from mingling. Machinery set, the press rolled. The test ran without further key adjustments and colors flowed steadily onto the paper. While a typical letterpress lays down a single color at a time, this split fountain machine laid down twenty-one colors.

Perfection, Larry thought, as the colored sheets rolled by.

Now it was time for its first real work. Done for an art paint manufacturer, the job, which would normally have required 16 passes through the press, was completed in just six passes without compromising the aesthetics. Larry realized he could generate almost three times the amount of work and three times the income for Pantone with this major time-saver.

The Levine brothers saw it differently and reported back to the client that because the job took less time to produce, they would cut the price in half.

Larry protested. "What did you do that for? He was happy with the price we gave him. We could have had the extra as profit." He continued his argument. "If you run two jobs at the price of one, you're gonna lose money. There's prepping and cleanup each time.

There's extra manpower involved here."

The Levines' flawed business decision, the first of many, raised Larry's hackles. *These guys have got to go*, he thought. The company had already lost many of their cosmetic clients to the salesman and color matcher who had left to start their own business. Secure with his process and knowing what it could do, Larry vowed to double Pantone's volume in one year from its sagging $150,000 — and he did. Among those clients who had defected and returned home was Revlon, who had apparently experienced color problems with the newly formed company. Revlon needed a rush job from its new printer. When they didn't perform up to speed, they turned to Larry knowing he could deliver the job in the specified time and without any problems. Larry assured Revlon that they would receive the job on time but would pay heavily for it.

Down the line, Revlon and others would benefit not only from Larry's dependability but from his ingenuity as well. When cosmetic companies began to introduce metallic-flecked colors, especially in nail polishes, the metals introduced into the inks settled before print application. The ink and metals were like oil and water, just not compatible. Stirring or shaking the bottles of metallics didn't do the trick either. Larry discovered a way to keep the metallics in constant suspension by using, of all things, a record turntable. One of the machinists mounted the turntable on its side, affixed pockets to hold the bottles of metallics, secured them, and then started the turntable up. At 33 1/3rd revolutions per minute, Larry was able to offer consistently correct metallic colors.

Nail polish displays mandating real metallic flecks and not just a metallic look presented another challenge and required a two-step operation. First, the colors, reds, pinks, corals, were printed onto the card stock. Then, while the ink remained damp, the sheets were moved into trays where hand-dusting a metallic chemical powder took place, after which they passed through a vacuuming facility. The result: a gold-flecked, glossy red, pink or coral nail polish look that was laminated and embossed between two die[15] stamp machines to complete the curved look for the displays.

The new press wasn't the only thing that Larry was birthing during that time. His first child, daughter Lisa, was due in November. Excited, Larry decided to buy a house, since he and his wife still maintained their studio apartment in Queens, quarters far too small for a growing family. They chose Rockland County, New York, for its

---

[15] *A die is a form, made in a particular shape to cut or bend an object into that shape.*

schools and friendly neighborhood feeling. The eight-room split-level house that appealed to the couple sat on a one-third acre comer lot. The price: $19,000. Calculating the monthly payments, Larry realized he could handle them on his salary of $155 a week, but he lacked the necessary $3,500 down payment. So he approached his bosses and discussed the matter.

Jesse and Mervyn Levine knew Larry was a sure bet. In a year and one-half, completely of his own initiative, he had instituted positive changes that had significantly increased the company's profit margin. His high-speed, split fountain press, the newly revamped ink selections, and his uncanny ability to manipulate and match colors had prompted a growth spurt for the company. Besides, the rock solid '50s projected continued economic and commercial growth, which promised increased business. The brothers agreed to the down payment, and although Larry offered to pay the $3,500 back, Jesse casually remarked, "Don't worry, we'll give you the down payment. You're worth it." The offhand comment led Larry to believe that the money was being given to him in lieu of a bonus. Unfortunately, the brothers, who unbeknownst to Larry had vehemently disagreed about many business-related issues all along, seemingly did not see eye-to-eye on this matter.

The Herberts moved into their new home and, with the help of friends and family, along with their living room and dinette pieces, furnished it with additional necessities, including the baby's room styled in white Italian Provincial. They had barely unpacked when

Jesse Levine surprised Larry by requesting a time frame for repayment of the money.

"What do you mean? I thought you gave me the money as a bonus!" Larry replied.

"Oh, no," said Levine. "It's a loan."

"But if it was a loan, why didn't you tell me that? I would never have purchased the house if I knew this. I just barely handle the payments as it is."

"Well, we'll give you a pay increase."

The increase, to the tune of $20 per week, did not even begin until the end of March 1958.

Jesse Levine walked away, leaving a stunned, and for the first time, speechless Larry in his wake.

5

Working It Out

On-the-job pressures mounted. After having lost cosmetic customers to the competition, Larry, already paid inadequately as printing foreman and color matcher, now acted as sole salesman responsible for bringing in new clients and filling the production voids. Moreover, when it came time to produce the jobs, he alone dealt with the clients' pickiness and demands.

Like all other printers in business, Larry also had to work with many ink manufacturers' color books in order to precisely match colors for his clients. His work ranged from featuring shades of face powder, nail polish and lipstick for Revlon, Helena Rubenstein and Max Factor to fine-tuning the degree of ripeness for strawberries and color gradation of walnuts for the U.S. Department of Agriculture, from discerning the variables in bacterial cultures for Squibb Pharmaceuticals to the clarity of vines for the California Wine Association. It was a laborious and complicated process at best. At worst, it was totally subjective.

THE KING *of* COLOR

Such was the case with Burlington Hosiery, an early Pantone client. Burlington bunched hosiery into peony-like puffs and photographed each piece for Larry to color match for their retail displays. An off-color match could easily result in lost sales for his client and a loss of client for him, making Larry particularly mindful of every task. At the point when Larry was ready to run the final job, after the test sheets had been viewed and initialed, Burlington's colorist came in and decided that the hosiery, which naturally covered a variety of beige tones, didn't look right. Larry tried to sort out the problem with prompts: Should it be redder? More yellow? Darker? Lighter?

No matter what direction he took, the difficulty, of course, lay in trying to make the color of three-dimensional fabric translate correctly into a two-dimensional image printed on paper, a task that even Houdini couldn't perform at the time.

Jobs like these created tension between client and printer. Larry spent endless hours hunched over the ink-mixing table, wasting valuable time he could have used securing much-needed new clients. Caught between that proverbial rock and hard place, his relationship with the Levine brothers also stretched to its limits. Finally, Burlington tried to drive one more nail in the coffin by asking for a discounted price on a completed and accepted job. Having learned from his father's mistakes and the Levines' tendency to backpedal, Larry preempted the Levines and stood his ground.

"It's full price or garbage." He added, "If the job is good enough to take at a discounted price, why isn't it good enough at full price?"

Point made.

Despite the recent loss of business, he chose to discontinue the relationship with Burlington.

Driven by the need for perfection, yet overworked, Larry returned to his mixing table to begin the next job. He looked up at the sign he had pinned above it some time back. The quote from Benjamin Disraeli read: *The secret of success in life is for a man to be ready for his Opportunity when it comes.* Larry breathed a heavy sigh.

Despite his frustration with a flawed system and the Levine brothers, Larry determined to stick it out, especially in view of the birth of his second daughter, Victoria. Pantone, he felt, was where opportunity lay, and Larry could make the most out of an opportunity. His new press enhanced Pantone's capacity and he knew it. He would find a new customer base. He would pursue the ink manufacturers to produce their color books for them — the very same books that he and other printers used.

By the turn of the decade, everywhere you looked, color was becoming more intense and vibrant. While the printing business burgeoned, many of the small ink manufacturers found it too costly to produce their own color charts. Larry knew he could produce quality books less expensively. He swung into action, but as a one-man show, his long hours introduced strife into his marriage. With an infant and young toddler both demanding all of her attention, Roberta could no longer attend functions with Larry in New York City, a source of frustration for the ambitious young printer. One can only imagine the resentment she must have felt about soloing on the parenting front. Career, however, took precedence.

Lewis Roberts, one of the largest ink manufacturers around, had created a massive color book called Match Master. A salesman of unparalleled skill, Larry approached the corporation once he had calculated the printing cost using a four-color press, including the time involved and the margin of color-match error versus his split fountain pricing. It was no contest. Larry's split fountain press made color charts affordable.

As Pantone's reputation grew, the company garnered more and more printing jobs. Like Revlon, even some of the old cosmetic manufacturers that had earlier jumped ship began to employ Pantone again. The pounding of the presses was music to Larry's ears. Money poured in...just not into Larry's bank account. He had his family to think of. Though money remained a constant concern for Larry, he had grown increasingly uncomfortable sharing his apprehensions with his wife. And though he thought about it unremittingly, he also didn't feel comfortable sharing his increasing resentment about the company's lack of profit-sharing.

Since doubling Pantone's sales to $300,000 in the first year the split fountain press was run, Larry had continued to create and cultivate major advantages for Pantone from which the Levine brothers profited handsomely.

He had even recreated his split fountain phenomenon on a more modern and impressive offset press, using the method he tried to convince Stuyvesant to switch to years earlier. That, too, had significantly boosted Pantone's profitability. The first job run on the new offset press brought in $42,000, while Pantone's costs remained a low $15,000.

Yet as quickly as Larry's innovations infused the company with money, the Levine brothers drained the funds, steadily withdrawing increasing amounts from the Press for their own use. While their pockets bulged, Larry's salary increases (including a few bonuses) inched along during this time, topping off at $15,000. Though Larry ran the show and did all the work, he had nothing to show for his efforts. He drove a 1952 pale blue Ford Customline in poor condition, which he had purchased secondhand in 1957. Though he had the house, he also had a loan and a mortgage hanging over his head. His increasing agitation with how the Levines ran the business prompted several friends to suggest that he leave Pantone and start his own company.

"The customers are yours. The technology is yours. We'll back you in business and that's that," he recalls one saying.

Reluctant to abandon the company into which he had invested so much of himself, he rejected the offer. The Levine brothers still owed him a raise for creating his offset version of the split fountain the year before. Finally, they delivered on their overdue promise to raise his weekly salary. They coughed up another $15 a week.

Larry had had enough. Disgusted and dismayed, he walked into Jesse's office that Friday and threw his paycheck and keys on the desk.

"I'm outta here. Right now," he barked. "I'd rather feel underpaid than insulted with this measly raise." Then he stomped out of the building.

Larry came to a decision while he stewed. A raise was no longer good enough. He deserved a share in the rewards spawned by his innovations — a very healthy share.

Arriving home that Friday evening, he said nothing to his wife about the day's events, instead focusing on the Mother's Day weekend with his three children: firstborn Lisa, middle child Victoria, and newborn son Richard. Family time was all too precious. Travel with three kids was limited to car rides to see grandparents and, when the weather heated, to the swim club nearby. On the long summer days, Larry liked to arrive home and mow the lawn while the children played outside. Because the house sat on a corner lot with nothing but field beyond, the dead end provided the kids with a safe area in which to play. No one but he drove up, so his occasional honk to the kids from the driveway clearly signaled his return home.

During easier times, Larry had even spent time building a split rail fence, painted it white, and bordered the property with Hemlock trees. Try as he might this weekend, however, he could not turn his mind away from work — or his possible lack thereof.

Silently, he mulled over his options, feeling certain the Levine brothers' need for him would force them to ask him back. As Monday morning rolled around, he broke the news to his wife that he had quit.

"Why would you do this? How are we going to live?" she asked nervously, thinking about their two daughters and newborn son.

"Unless I'm mistaken, by 10:30 a.m. I'll get a call."

He was wrong. He didn't receive a call until noon when Pantone's accountant, Lou Coleman, phoned. More than anyone, Lou knew just how integral Larry had been to the company's financial turnaround. Pleading with Larry to open a dialogue, he said, "I know they are willing to do something to get you back Larry."

"Lou, I changed their technology and increased their business and got nothing," Larry shot back. "I was due a raise and they put it off. I run sales, pre-press production, production and post-production. I'm doing everything for Pantone Press, and they're just sitting back and smiling all the way to the bank." Then Larry unleashed the Rottweiler in him. "What I want is fifty percent ownership of Pantone Press, and I don't want to pay a penny for it."

"Let me talk to them. I'll get back to you," said Lou.

Knowing that the Levines would continue to make money under the newly proposed arrangement, Lou strongly advised the brothers to make a deal. "Without Larry establishing new business, you might as well close the doors," he asserted.

The negotiations continued for the next few days. The Levines countered with twenty-five percent of the net profits.

"It's no deal," Larry retorted. "I can't control net profits."

They upped their offer to forty percent.

The headstrong negotiator stood his ground. He required complete control over the Press's income: no money would fund the

Levine's other ventures.

"It's half of Pantone Press or nothing," he demanded.

On Thursday of that week, Larry and his attorney, a friend and neighbor who offered his help, strolled into the office of the Levines' attorney to sign papers. The next day, as president and co-owner of Pantone Press, a new era began that would prove both challenging and lucrative.

Larry had instituted some ground-breaking changes at Pantone Press from 1956 to 1962, but there was still work to be done as president. Flawed inks from a multitude of manufacturers and the inability to consistently match colors remained a thorn. Moreover, the type of problem he experienced with Burlington occurred time and again, convincing him that standardizing color was the only solution for an industry thrust into chaos. Carl Foss, who co-consulted for the Container Corporation of America, had introduced Larry to the Color Marketing Group, a small concern that worked to offer color uniformity across industries. Though he remained skeptical about whether the ink industry would commit to such revolutionary upheaval in their business practices, being labeled 'just a printer' wasn't reward enough for Larry. Along with affluence, he craved acceptance and recognition from his peers.

A leader and not a follower, Larry burned to excel. His chance came in 1962 at the Ink Makers' Convention, held in Santa Barbara, California. The conference provided Larry with a clearer insight into the inner workings and politics of the ink manufacturing business. A cliquish group, with an edge of superiority, they managed to keep outsiders at arm's length. All but one, that is.

When Larry discussed the idea that he had played out in his mind so many times with ink manufacturer Vince Subenski, he found a common ground: possibility.

"Lar, it's possible," Vince replied, aiming his chubby finger to emphasize his next point. "It's gotta happen sooner or later. This industry can't continue on the way it's going."

"Vince, how am I going to get these cockeyed guys to come on board?" Larry responded, giving voice to his most pressing concern. "If I rattle their cages too hard, they'll put me out of business."

Vince recognized that Larry had the ability and knowledge to find a solution that could pull an expanding, yet increasingly fragmented, industry together. "Go for it, Larry. I'll back you 100 percent."

The ink manufacturer knew from personal experience just what kind of opposition Larry would face. Years before, he had attempted to create a standardized color system but shelved his efforts when he could not bring other ink manufacturers into the fold. Consensus did not come naturally to them.

Why the difference now? Color was big business. Printing was big business because advertising was big business because consumerism was big business. *TIME* magazine in its October 12, 1962, issue had even referred to advertising's top twelve men as "The Visible Persuaders" and announced that "'Madison Avenue,' the all-purpose handle for the advertising business, is a street named Desire that starts in Manhattan and wends into every household in the land."

In the hopes that Larry could deliver where he had failed, Vince handed Larry his rudimentary plan. "Rework it. Refine it. Do whatever you want to it. Once you create the basics and come up with an acceptable standard for designers and their clients, I'll help you make it applicable to ink manufacturers." Then he pushed his glasses up to the bridge of his nose.

This was all the impetus Larry needed. He innately understood the potential impact this system could have on the industry. The spread of offset printing had forced the development of newer, thinner, intensely pigmented inks. Clearly, the printing industry governed the ink industry. Nevertheless, his universal color matching system would force manufacturers and printers to work hand-in-hand.

Larry silently calculated the money-making potential of his plan and determined that the Levine brothers would not share in his newest idea. He would work alone and wait for the right opportunity.

By early 1963, parent company Pantone Inc. lay in shambles. The brothers had received their half share from Larry's profitable printing division and continued to pour it into their hemorrhaging advertising display division. As president of Pantone Press, the monthly business reports Larry received from the accountant gave him ammunition. Continued agitation with the Levines gave him determination. No longer willing to put his innovations to work for them or to put up with their obstructive business decisions, he wanted them out —

permanently.

It was time to strike. Larry seized the moment. The no-interest, handshake-only loan from Elsie had put her attorney unexpectedly on notice. He called a meeting with the two at Elsie's home. The attorney began to question Larry extensively while Elsie looked on. Larry explained the system idea and reiterated his promise to pay Elsie back in one year. "There's only one thing about the deal I don't like," he added.

"What is that," asked the attorney.

"She won't take interest from me!"

The loan that Elsie Williamson gave him that April morning in 1962 allowed him to buy the Press division outright with continued financial obligations to the brothers into 1964 and continue his quest for a unified color system. By fulfilling his self-imposed mission, he would not only find the pot of gold at the end of the rainbow, he would grab the rainbow itself.

THE KING *of* COLOR

6

Creating the International Language of Color

Like 'grasping a handful of water',[16] controlling the rainbow defies all reason — a concept not lost on Larry. Neither was the fact that the printing industry in the early 1960s was in a state of chaos and flux, about to face future shock.

Color had exploded onto the consumer scene. The tempestuous split-personality of the 60s spawned commercialized color TV and the Age of Aquarius, daisy prints and embroidered jeans, the mop-top Beatles and big hair, barely-there hemlines and go-go boots. Powerful, fluorescent DayGlo® colors displaced pallid 50s palettes. Sex, drugs and rock and roll eclipsed family values, while *TIME* magazine asked: "Is God Dead?"

Color TV, though invented in the 1940s and introduced into the marketplace in the 1950s, didn't take hold until the 1960s.

[16] *Joseph Conrad quoted in The Midnight Disease (New York: Publisher 2003), 81.*

THE KING *of* COLOR

THE COLOR ASSOCIATION OF THE U.S.

In 1915, nearly five decades before the PANTONE
MATCHING SYSTEM, the Textile Card Association
of the U.S., initiated by Margaret Hayden Rourke,
promoted color coordination among various textile
trades. It introduced colors by word code and number,
but not by formulas. In 1955, it changed its name to
the Color Association of the U.S. (and remains so today)
and involved itself in color forecasting, but never
ventured into the area of ink pigments or printing.

Consistent growth in color programming became the catalyst for the
demand for color televisions. "Madison Avenue" had become
all-powerful. Names like Ogilvy, Benson & Mather; Doyle Dane
Bernbach; Foote, Cone & Belding; J. Walter Thompson; Leo
Burnett, Inc.; Young & Rubicam; Ted Bates & Co., and some 500
other advertising agencies in the U.S. of varying sizes, perpetuated an
average of 1600 ads per person per day in newspapers, magazines, on
billboards and, increasingly, on television. Television, as J. Walter
Thompson's president Norman Strouse put it "...makes it possible
for advertisers to impose rudely on the viewer," prompting companies
like Ted Bates & Co. to funnel 80 percent of its ad budget into television advertising. Boomer families with postwar offspring initiated

into TV-dom remained loyal worshippers.

What better way to mesmerize the masses into consumerism? During cartoon shows, every child was goaded into demanding the newest toy; breaks during sitcoms and other family shows induced a fascination with all things youthful; ads proclaimed a romantic, sexier image when touting products that whitened teeth, groomed hair or provided a cleaner shave. Color, the most powerful advertising aid, gave life to recognizable images: the he-man with the tan, the blond actress with the red lipstick, the tantalizing food we hoped to put on our tables, the cars we bought or coveted, even the cigarettes we smoked. Each bit of persuasion came to us in vivid color.

Though the counter-culture movement would grab the world by a choke-hold during the latter 1960s, trying to turn everything on its head, it never stomped the life out of the economy. Instead, the movement effectively breathed life into the marketplace. Madison Avenue embraced its quirkiness and brought it to the masses, plying us with peace, love and psychedelic colors.

With this, color developed into an increasingly critical tool for marketing. Reimagined ad campaigns based on psychedelic rock art posters shook up staid notions of advertising and created a hip, irreverent capitalist revolution. Helen Gurley Brown recognized this upheaval with Emilio Pucci's brightly colored designs. "Magenta, bright blue, gold, flamingo, acid green, pink, peach…I once counted fifteen different colors in a Pucci peignoir and nightgown set."

Even before this upheaval, change in the realm of color prompted forward-thinking ad agencies to provide new support services to their clients. Advising them on product, packaging and merchandising, they backed their ideas with researched statistics, economists and psychologists — all in the name of commercialism.

Ironically, color, a key component at the center of the hullabaloo, remained a hit-or-miss proposition for Madison Avenue ad agencies. Ad men turned into madmen as carefully formulated campaigns turned into a horse of a different color depending on the kind of media used or the geographic region where the campaign was printed. Given that every single print shop continued to custom-mix its own colors, a peaches-and-cream complexion could easily morph into a sunburn or a colorless geisha look depending on the idiosyncrasies of the printer.

Though President Kennedy considered 1961 the "valley of the recession,"[17] by 1962, recovery and growth filled the American spirit. Yet, while men could be launched into space, printers still could not sufficiently match ink colors.

Larry continued to print color cards for the ink manufacturers in order to maintain his status within the industry and provide solid business flow. Larry's popular offset technique helped boost his ratings with Karl Anton of Van Son Holland Ink Company. Carl sought out and supplied inks to the smaller printers for whom he

---

[17] *Transcript of the President's Address to Congress on Domestic and World Affairs, New York Times; Jan 12, 1962; ProQuest Historical Newspapers The New York Times (1851-2002), pg 12.*

provided color cards. The project, he showed Larry, consisted of a mere twelve colors placed on one card, but he wanted one hundred thousand cards! The mild-mannered man then asked Larry for a quote on the job. Larry's figure came to six cents a card, totaling $6,000. Karl showed no surprise but told Larry that his budget couldn't exceed $4,000. There was only one reason for Larry to consider this lower price: Karl's customers, the small presses. Having the cards distributed this expansively, Larry knew, would someday be in his best interest. It was. Karl and Larry became the best of friends until Karl's dying day. Karl supported the color system and even suggested that Larry place a retail value on the books themselves. He also financially backed Larry around 1968 when the color maven overextended himself in the production of ancillary products and sat on a large inventory of fan books.

More importantly, the ongoing printing work allowed Larry to repay Elsie Williamson back within the time he had stipulated. On the 364th day following her loan to him, Larry took Elsie to lunch near her office. Nothing elegant or fancy, just a place on 57th Street she liked. The two sat facing each other and picked up their menus. "Let's get this thing out of the way," insisted Larry as he handed her a check for $50,000. "Now, let's have lunch."

He didn't try to talk her into accepting interest, knowing from many previous attempts that she would refuse. Instead, he hatched another plan. Knowing Elsie had planned to purchase a new car, he drove to the Cadillac dealer some time later and asked who handled

Mrs. Williamson's account.

"I do," replied a stout man.

"Well, good. I want to pay for Mrs. Williamson's car," declared Larry.

"Oh, you must be Mr. Herbert," stated the man. "Mrs. Williamson left explicit instructions that we were not to take your money, no matter how much you insisted."

Larry, who had thought he had been so smart and so cunning, burst out laughing and walked out of the dealership.

Though it provided a good livelihood, Larry had long since realized that the custom color books and charts he printed for the ink manufacturers only exacerbated the confusion. Each company maintained its own color chart and proprietary color book, causing designers whiplash-speed headaches as they had to switch charts with almost every job, and printers to carry the obligatory color books from manufacturers A through Z to ensure quality control.

As far as Larry was concerned, the cumbersome process was a mess, but one he surely could fix. Furthermore, smaller ink makers, at the mercy of the industry's bigger guns, encouraged him to come up with a workable solution. With the enthusiastic support ink manufacturer Vince Subenski echoing in his brain, Larry sequestered he and his staff in his laboratory and furiously began to mix inks and proof each of the colors. Over time, they gathered some 9,500 color proofs, then plunged into researching the commercial use of color.

As a prime source for manufacturing the color charts and books for ink manufacturers, Larry assumed that his reputation at the center of the ink industry would give him access to key decision-makers and heads of production in a range of businesses. He was right. From General Printing Ink to Seaboard, clients and non-clients shared their frustrations and problems. They all told the same tales of woe. The cost of producing large color books had become exorbitant. A completed book often took up to six months to produce (compared to Larry's one month to print and two weeks to bind), all the while tying up a tech person who could otherwise be used in the laboratory. Further, with demand for color printing on an all-time rise and the cost of printing in color considered precious, mistakes began to eat into profits.

It didn't take a genius to figure out that the lack of color consistency lay at the root of the problem. It would, however, take a visionary to come up with a solution — a universal color system.

Well-acquainted with all the other color systems, their histories and their uses, Larry knew that not one of them would work as the building blocks for his system. Infringement, too, was a concern. Larry had to create a "new" product that didn't use any of the colors formulated by anyone else if he didn't want to share the profits with untold numbers of ink manufacturers. That meant that pigment selection for Larry's system would have to be built from the ground up.

Moving from problem to solution, Larry delved into the dizzying world of research twenty-four/seven.

First he determined which colors — and shades of those colors — were the most popular. Though the 1950s had sported pinks, pastels and even turquoise, he knew these weren't popular printing colors. So he returned to basics and surveyed the pigment manufacturers to discover the most frequently ordered color pigments. By far, the most often called for had been red, followed by blue and green. Black and yellow followed. Purple made an appearance along with brown and orange.

Brown, since it does not appear on the color wheel, is considered by color chemists as dirty orange, but the color family called orange comes in many shades. As a secondary color, made by mixing red and yellow pigments, it enjoys the characteristics of both colors. Its associations run the gamut from stimulating and aggressive to bright and cheerful. Artist Vassily Kandinsky said of the color, "orange is like a man, convinced of his own powers."[18]

Once Larry had determined which pigments were most popular according to the suppliers, he matched his findings with those most widely used by designers. Again, he found reds and blues had been most often used.

"After substantial research with the colors and the strengths of these pigments, I chose a certain set of pigments that would satisfy all the requirements," Larry recalls.

Oddly, the first selection of pigments did not include orange

---

[18] *Kandinsky, Concerning The Spiritual in Art, Dover Publ. New York 1977, translated by M.T.H. Sadler.*

INK DURABILITY

Testing the viscosity and durability of ink is conducted with a "water pickup" test. As printing plates are dampened by a rolled-on solution containing water during the printing process, the water integrates into the oil-based inks. Increased amounts of water break down the ink, which "grays out." The dampening solution begins to transfer ink particles to non-print areas, creating scum, and diminishing print.

Though many systems displayed the color, according to Larry, the lack of demand for orange in printing during the '60s did not justify including orange in the primary palette. Though considered a hot color in some arenas, and considered by the likes of Frank Sinatra to be "the happiest color," it was generally associated with cheapness. Larry's decision would unwittingly help promulgate the end of business for one pigment manufacturer who supplied orange exclusively. Not until the development of subsequent systems would Larry add the color to his primary palette. Ironically, the color he originally shunned would become so popular decades later that Ford, in conjunction with hip Australian designer Mare Newson, would name its urban concept car, displayed at the Tokyo Motor Show in 1999, 021C after the PANTONE Shade of orange.

With a baseline of pigments selected for mixing, it was time to begin building the system Larry had carried around in his head for so long. He hired both an ink technician and an assistant to sort the color swatches: reds, blues, greens, yellows, etc. As the stacks grew, Larry queried designers and art directors again. He displayed the color ranges before them and asked for feedback. "What's missing here that you would like to see?" he enquired.

"More reds. We need more reds," they asserted. For presentations, red 'popped.' Its dramatic nature drew the consumer's attention and sent an energizing message. Before DayGlo hit the consumer scene in the latter part of the '60s, red was the definitive color used in design.

After Larry had gathered and categorized the 9,500 color proofs and sampled color users, he stopped the process. "It's enough. It's unworkable. Let's step back and narrow it to a range of basic mid-value colors."

At this point, Larry's expertise as a pressman kicked in. "We need to consider the press tolerance level," he pointed out, knowing that colors too similar to one another could not be controlled on the press and so would have to be eliminated. The human eye's capability of recognizing minute variations in color values does not translate to the printing press: a little more or less ink on the press would result in the next color step. Only exactness would do.

Using a method akin to fingerprinting, Larry marked points of similarity among the mid-line colors: some colors, too close in value, were removed. He even went so far as to create new basic shades, unique to Pantone, from the industry standards Rhodamine red and Rhodamine purple, synthetic inks with fluorescent qualities that added to the color brilliance. Larry requested that his pigment provider remove 5 percent of the Rhodamine red and 5 percent of the Rhodamine purple and mix them with the other, changing each color visibly and technically enough so as not to be considered the same base colors as others had used.

With several ranges of colors chosen, Larry moved on to the next phase in creating the color matching system — the elimination of redundancies. Palettes were reduced according to color preferences. He discovered, for instance, that designers didn't require an inordinate number of purples, which seemed to emerge only seasonally in product promotion, but loved reds. So he maintained a smaller purple palette and increased the red palette but only insofar as technical feasibility allowed reproduction on the press. Working diligently, he and his technicians, Gus Lindquist and Mike Garin, further reduced the number of baseline colors to 200.

From this selection, each color was tinted with white to create three lighter versions, and shaded with black to create three darkened variations. That resulted in 1,400 colors. That many formulations meant a cumbersome book rather than a narrow fan-style book. Already used by some ink manufacturers, like Glenn-Killian, Lewis Roberts, and IPI, at that time, Larry knew the fan-style book could be easily grasped and held in one hand, as long as it was small enough.

"This thing has to be manageable. Reduce it," ordered Larry. "Our target is five hundred colors."

Larry had already calculated the number of colors per page as seven: one mid-line color plus three tints and three shades. Seventy-one, two-inch wide, card-weight pages would display the nearly five hundred bands of color. His target number wasn't random either. The major ink manufacturers had presented that many, and Larry understood that to remain competitive, he would have to do the same. So, from eight basic colors, plus black and transparent mixing white, Larry and his team devised the first PANTONE MATCHING SYSTEM.

While color reduction progressed in the hands of Gus and Larry's brother-in-law, Mike Garin, Larry turned his attention to his marketing strategy. He had major concerns that needed to be addressed: How much would someone be willing to spend on a color book? Whom should he target first? How would he approach them? The answers lay in his knowledge of the industry. He would begin his campaign directed at the core of the industry's problems — the ink manufacturers. To elicit orders in multiples from the manufacturers, Larry recognized that the book had to be practically priced to warrant ink manufacturers giving up their own books and using his to give to their customers, the printers.

Of the hundreds of ink manufacturers across the U.S., Larry identified twenty-one aggressive, up-and-coming, mid-size companies. He sat down to compose a letter explaining the system and its benefits. *You're spending a lot of money producing your own color books, which will be obsolete by the time you use them.* He continued his plea. *I'm offering an opportunity that will come at a reasonable price.* As added insurance, he pointed out that he had been consulting with a well-respected manufacturer in the ink industry. With little money to spare, Larry worked with, of all people, Jesse Levine, whose agency helped create copy, lay out brochures and pull together the first full-page launch ad geared to the ink manufacturers. Larry then ran prototype sample fans, packed them with the letters, and mailed all twenty-one.

Within days the phone rang.

"Who's this guy you're working with?" demanded the voice on the line.

"Vince Subenski of Seaboard Ink Company."

"Good. We just want to make sure it's not one of the big guys, and you're not just shoving their system down everyone's throats."

Acquainting himself with the man behind the voice, Larry patiently explained that all five hundred colors were based on eight basic pigments plus transparent mixing white and black. After reviewing how he had created the system, he described how color matching would be controlled through standard formulations.

"It's about time we had some leverage against the big companies," replied the voice.

Larry knew word would spread quickly.

Since purchasing Pantone and initiating his idea, work for Larry had become even more all-encompassing than before. While the system moved toward finalization, and the sales letter with dummy fans were made ready to roll, Larry traveled to Colorado Springs to promote his idea at the Ink Manufacturers Convention held at the Broadmoor Hotel in spring 1963. His time at home had dwindled since acquiring Pantone and vacations were out of the question now, so he used this as an opportunity for Roberta to get away, knowing that his sales manager's wife would be accompanying him. At the convention, some 280 companies in any ink-related business attended, including ink industry big guns like Flint and Superior, who today count themselves among loyal PANTONE MATCHING SYSTEM devotees.

Ink manufacturers at the conference, particularly those in charge of color books and with systems of their own, remained unconvinced of the need for a singular color matching system by which they would all have to abide and stood divided on Larry's concept. One by one, Larry met members, introduced himself, and explained the PANTONE MATCHING SYSTEM — specific formulas that allowed anyone, anywhere, to select and print the same colors simply by referring to the book and stocking eight ink colors on their shelf. His idea, he continued, permitted the smaller guys to play on the same level with the larger ink manufacturers.

The mom-and-pop operations loved it. The big ink manufacturers, on the other hand, simply wanted to have him shot.

At the industry Board of Directors meeting, the young, brash 'printer' touting his new color system Copped the agenda. The ink manufacturers had a way of keeping suppliers and anyone else at arms' length, beyond their inner circle. Larry had already felt notably unwelcome at the event, when he, his new salesman and their wives were treated in a manner bordering on rudeness, something Roberta could not quite understand not having been in the workplace. When Larry tried to introduce himself to one ink manufacturer, the conversation was abruptly ended. Another excused himself. Still others simply ignored him. Word had apparently spread to discount Larry, the intruder. Larry took all of this in stride. Roberta, on the other hand, couldn't understand why Larry would put up with their arrogance and wished she had never come. "It's all part of the business," he remarked. "If you want to get ahead, you have to make sacrifices." Larry forged on. Later that day, as he joined others to greet Bob Flint and introduced himself, Flint irresolutely responded, "Oh, Mr. Herbert." *At least they know my name now*, he thought to himself.

The next day, Larry hosted a cocktail party in his suite, attended by then president of Superior Ink Company, Nat Rosen, who had come to question the intruder.

"Herbert, you know what's going on, don't you? The manufacturers feel that this system of yours will ruin the industry. It will make ink a commodity."

85

As if it wasn't already, Larry thought.

"It may take the wind out of some of your sails, Nat, but the system can only help," Larry retorted. "And not only the ink industry, but others, too."

"It's a big mistake, Larry. Don't put out this system," Rosen furthered in a formidable tone. "The board will do everything possible to prevent you from doing this."

Though not one to back down, Larry replied, "Let me think about it, Nat."

Larry had clearly rattled the ink manufacturers' cages. He now had to win them over. If his idea was ever going to fly, he would have to take on the Ink Manufacturers of America and convince them to adopt his new standardized color system.

To kick off that campaign, he flew directly from Colorado Springs to Denver to meet with Max Clarkson, chairman of the Printing Industries of America, and attend their annual meeting.

While engaged in discussion, Max Clarkson reassured him. "Don't these people realize that they are nothing but suppliers to us? If they think they are going to tell us printers what to do, they have another thing coming."

"Can I count on your backing?" asked Larry.

"If it's good for the industry, Larry, we'll back you one hundred Percent."

Just the words Larry wanted to hear.

Tensions rose among the ink manufacturers. Some, like Sinclair, became highly vocal in their fight against the plan. Larry knew the only way to make his venture bulletproof was to spread the word — as fast as possible. Time an enemy now, he raced to finish his system and get a healthy number of ink makers to adopt the PANTONE MATCHING SYSTEM before the biggest players united and offered a solution of their own. He played his trump card and placed a simple, stark, clean, black and white ad in *American Ink Maker* magazine simply stating, "The PANTONE MATCHING SYSTEM will be delivered September 30." The underscored word "will" suggested that the ink makers not toy with Larry Herbert.

Larry fielded every question regarding the soon-to-premiere PANTONE MATCHING SYSTEM and discussed his terms. "If you want to join," he told them, "I want fifty percent down in advance."

Within three weeks, 20 of the 21 ink manufacturers in receipt of Larry's letter had placed orders, a tact and response that astounded the laid-back Jesse Levine. Quickly, Larry mailed more letters and fan-style samples, and just as quickly gained more supporters. By the time the finished product shipped, 32 manufacturers with multiple branches had signed on under the original plan, giving Larry the national coverage in 130 locations he needed. Most of those early subscribers would turn into lifelong Pantone customers.

California Ink Company's Advertising Manager, Randy Cook, though already very familiar with Larry's ingenuity, did not hale as one of the first to take advantage of the new system, a bombshell to Larry since their prior working relationship had been solid. Cook, burdened like so many other ink manufacturers with having to offer an expansive color chart that took nearly six months to produce, approached Larry to do the job. To secure the business, Larry proposed to produce Cook's chart in six days — or it would be free. Cook couldn't believe his ears.

"It can't be done!"

Larry smiled and shrugged. "Well, what have you got to lose?" Cook took the challenge. Larry first set up 25 colors on his split fountain press, proofed them in three different values, and sent the proofs overnight to California by Emery Air Freight. While waiting on press, he asked Cook to select and phone his choices by number, and then printed the final version. The next day, he ran 25 more colors and proceeded the same way. By the sixth day, Cook had his color charts in his warehouse.

"I would never have believed something like this was possible," the company's vice president commented at the next ink manufacturers' conference.

"It's my process that makes it so fast," explained Larry with a notable sense of satisfaction and pride.

Randy Cook became a good friend. Producing his company's color books made him a good client. Nonetheless, affected by the directors at the Broadmoor meeting whose influence lingered, Cook hesitated to join others who adopted the PANTONE MATCHING

SYSTEM. Immediately following the initial Pantone shipment, offered at $2.50 per book, Larry raised the price to $3.00. When Randy Cook called soon after, Larry thought he had a convert. Instead, he stunned Larry with news.

"California Ink wants to put out its own system, like Pantone's, and they want you to print it for them."

"I'm not going to do it for you," Larry said with resolve. "I can, but I won't."

"Why? It's a $50,000 job," quizzed Cook.

"I know, but I value friendship more than the $50,000. You've been good to me, Randy," Larry asserted. "You're making a big mistake. Don't do it. The industry is moving the Pantone way. Rather than spend $50,000, just order 1,000 PANTONE MATCHING SYSTEM Books. It will only cost you $3,000."

Larry hit a nerve — the bottom line — a factor in any business. Finally, Cook came to his senses.

`Yeah, you can't go wrong this way," he agreed. He ordered 1,000 books and has never looked back.

By October 1963, with the first books in hand, the swell had begun. Naysayers, like Nat Rosen of Superior Ink, finally realized the cost of their own books was simply too prohibitive. One by one, afraid to lose their competitive edge, they hopped on board. Only a few ink manufacturers, who considered Larry an outsider — and just a printer — with no right to dictate to the ink makers, remained bitter. But Larry offered more than a two-inch wide, fan-shaped book pinioned with a post. He offered service. Formulas and spectropho-tometric color readings accompanied each of the colors for perfect color matching. For those who still wanted to produce the basic colors themselves, he offered sources. PMS® (the acronym for the PANTONE MATCHING SYSTEM) as the system was first known, proved a foolproof tool for communication.

As it turned out, the acronym PMS was a registered trademark held by a company called Plastic Molders Supply. In 1963, they issued a cease and desist to Pantone to stop using the acronym. Although individuals continued to refer to the PANTONE MATCHING SYSTEM as PMS, the company never again promoted the system by the acronym. In the mid-1980s, when Plastic Molders Supply let their trademark lapse, Larry registered it as his own.

Be that as it may, the PANTONE MATCHING SYSTEM proved a win-win situation for designers, printers and ink manufac-turers. It wouldn't be until twenty-five years later, at opening night at the Metropolitan Opera, that Nat Rosen would comment to Larry, "I know I've been a pain-in-the-ass for a lot of years, but I have to compliment you on the tremendous job you have done for the industry by coming up with a color system that everybody could use."

Business finally seemed to progress smoothly. Customers now comfortable with the system became loyal users. Though Larry had raised his price from $2.50 a book to $3.00, his client base contin-ued to grow. The industry furor had calmed. Then Edgar Flint of Flint Ink Company called.

CADMIUM

*Though discovered in 1817 by Franz Stromeyer, the
cadmium substance was not incorporated into paints
made commercially available until 1840. In 1842, the
middle yellow to light orange cadmium sulfide was
marketed followed by lighter yellows, which incorporated
zinc sulfide (since cadmium and zinc deposits are
generally found in ores near one another). Further
manipulation of cadmium with selenium resulted in
deeper oranges, bright reds and deep reds. The patented
results (1892) became the basis for artists' paints in 1910.*

*Cadmium toxicity became an issue when the
introduction of mercury in 1948 created the compound,
cadmium mercury sulfide, which no longer remains in
use commercially.*

*The luminous, highly saturated quality and richness
of cadmium colors resides in the fact that the pure
substance reflects no blue light. Used by fine artists and
considered too expensive for general printing because
of the process by which they are created, Cadmiums
were out-placed by the invention of synthetics.*

"Larry, come to Detroit. Carl Jacobsen, my v.p. of marketing and
I want to talk to you about buying the books."

Assuming he would deliver his standard sales pitch and ring up
another new client, Larry never considered that there was a problem.
The next day, he flew into Detroit for the meeting. He sat across an

expansive wooden desk facing Edgar Flint, with Carl Jacobsen to his left. The window's glare behind Flint dissipated as the formidable man leaned onto his forearms to speak, his tan face and neatly combed sandy hair clearly visible now.

"These books, Herbert, I'll buy five thousand of them from you, but I don't want to pay $3.00 a book. I want to pay $2.50 a book."

"Mr. Flint, the price is $3.00 a book," Larry replied, showing the resolve that had shaped his career to date.

"I want to pay $2.50," scowled the elder gentleman. "Take it or leave it."

Disappointed, Larry explained that he could certainly use the money, but he wasn't about to taint his reputation in the industry by underselling to anyone. He prided himself on treating every ink company the same. Flint abruptly ended the meeting.

"Okay. There's nothing more to talk about Herbert."

Larry returned home. The next morning, Carl Jacobsen called, elated. "Larry, the best thing you could have done was to stand up to Flint. He may be hardheaded, but he's a 'no BS' kind of guy and he saw the same in you. He liked your ethical stance. He says he'll take the five thousand books at $3.00 each. When can we get them?"

Larry sat back and savored his journey. When he had acquired Pantone from the Levine brothers, the company had only seven employees — three printing pressmen, one color matcher, one production supervisor, a bookkeeper and a receptionist — and his innovative split fountain press. Over the years, Larry had functioned as the sole sales staff, while still wearing his pressman's hat. He remained the only one who could print critically matched color cards for the cosmetic industry, the medical field, the Gemological Society, agricultural companies and more. All precision work and all requiring innovative thinking and resolve.

To develop the blood anemia charts for Clay Adams, for example, Larry researched a series of pigments that could maintain color consistency and long-term permanency on the charts. Ultimately, he decided to work with the cadmiums — orange, red and yellow — long used by artists and known for their high color saturation, opacity, light-fastness and stability when used industrially in temperatures over 3000 degrees Celsius.

As letterpress surrendered to web offset for the nation's newspapers, and as news of Larry's problem-solving prowess spread, even the Newspaper Association of America turned to Larry when Pall Mall cigarette ads ranged in color from a positively unmanly pale pink to an unappealing dark maroon across the country, a costly mistake in more ways than one. In response, Larry worked with the NAA's Specifications for Newsprint Advertising Production (SNAP) guidelines to help set a printing standard with a color matching book designed specifically for the accurate reproduction of color on newsprint. Called the Run of Press (ROP), the system — initiated just after the introduction of the PANTONE MATCHING SYSTEM — worked for both letterpress and offset production and is still used to this day. Indeed, ROP, along with further prepress

COLOR SIGNATURES

Color is a critical component in retail sales. Though very few firms have been able to register color alone as their trademark since color became a marketing tool around 1945, it clearly helps to distinguish a company or brand. TIME *magazine sets itself apart on the shelf from other weeklies by bordering the cover in red. An interesting adjunct, discussing the issue of printing, appears in* TIME *magazine's July 25, 1927, "Letter to the Editor" and reads:*

SIRS: IN YOUR LETTER COLUMN — JULY 4 — G.H. GREENE AND J.W. VANDER REFER TO TIME'S ORANGE BORDER AS "RED." IT IS ORANGE, ISNT IT — OR AM I COLOR BLIND? -HARRIET INGERSOLL, SAINT PAUL, MINN.

TO WHICH THE EDITOR REPLIES:
"THE BORDER IS RED. BUT THE RED INK IS PRINTED OVER YELLOW. EXPOSURE TO MUCH DAMPNESS OR SUNLIGHT WOULD FADE IT ORANGE. HOW TO SAY WHERE ORANGE ENDS, WHERE RED BEGINS?"

When we shop, we may not notice a brand's colors: our awareness and recall have become so ingrained that we take for granted the red and white Campbell's soup can, the green Fuji film box, the Lucky Strike cigarette red circle, the green disk with the Starbuck's mermaid, the informational Yellow Pages, and Colgate's red toothpaste box. But those color choices seriously impact our purchasing decisions. When Target switched its signature red bulls eye, which draws shoppers to the popular retailer without even mentioning the company's name, to teal, sales figures plummeted.
    So successful has been brand identity linked to color that many of those companies 'own' their colors in their respective categories. If we feel like we are bombarded with color, well, we are. Manufacturers and their advertising agencies have long known that color is the most effective way to communicate to consumers.

technology, is what made possible the introduction of full-color newspapers in 1982, which finally gave newspapers an edge against color TV.

Once criticized as merely a printer, Larry — inventor, wizard and master of color — was well on his way to becoming the color industry's superstar. With his newly acquired company still in its infancy, he laid down plans for the future. He would expand Pantone into an international system and promote it as the dominant color language. However, it would cost him.

THE KING *of* COLOR

7

Expanding the Empire

Like a conductor, Larry began to orchestrate the individual instruments of color into a melody heard worldwide. At an informational meeting for Capital Printing Ink in Washington, D.C., in 1964, the meeting chairman praised Larry's hard work and contributions and introduced him as the man who had created a color empire, owned the rainbow, and put Pantone on the globe by creating, along with Morse Code and Semaphore, one of only three international codes. But success came at a price.

Though the Levine Brothers were completely out of the picture by 1964, Larry would continue to suffer the effects of their mismanagement. Pantone, Inc., the umbrella company, had incorporated both the advertising display division (Levine Advertising) and the press (Pantone Press). While the press grew and profited, the advertising display division had declined. Even when Larry had dropped the display division, along with the name Pantone 'Press,' the trail of debts left behind, including payments due on prior owners Jesse and

THE KING *of* COLOR

Mervyn Levine's notes for printing equipment, which Larry had agreed to clean up, placed a drain on the foundling Pantone, Inc.

Still, the PANTONE MATCHING SYSTEM continued to sweep through the printing industry like a firestorm even when the price eventually rose to $15 a book. Yet, in the process that sparked more than a few problems for Larry, not the least of which was the issue of violation of his system, Larry understood that such tactics were simply part of doing business, even though this really amounted to theft. He also understood that if he didn't protect his turf, the pot at the end of his rainbow would shrink considerably.

While Larry shored up his business against possible erosion and outright piracy, he continued to build it and assumed the sales mantle that he would wear for the next fifteen years. Like a gospel preacher spreading the Pantone word, he sold the system to whomever would stop long enough to listen to his *schpiel*. "Look, the major ink manufacturers have you at a disadvantage. They've all put out their own big color books making you look small just because you can't afford the expense of printing your own. If you use my color system, you can buy a minimum number of books at a fraction of the cost of producing your own books."

As his client base began to swell, Larry realized that he had to expand his horizons and look for new avenues of growth. But how and where? These questions would eventually be answered in 1967 by a man he had hired the prior year.

Around the time Larry began his system, Sinclair and Valentine

Ink Company was one of the larger ink manufacturers in the U.S. with yet another color book. Once on board, the ink company, a die-hard opponent of the new system, would maintain a business relationship with Larry for years to come.

Though the relationship with the Sinclair and Valentine would eventually become strained, Larry would profit from the affiliation in a completely different way as well. When the company changed presidents in 1966, their international sales representative, Rudy Gothman, decided to leave the company and approached Larry for a job. Rudy brought extensive sales knowledge and all the right foreign contacts. Recognizing this as his opportunity for global expansion, Larry hired him.

Rudy immediately began traveling to Europe and South America to set up accounts and quickly became Pantone's catalyst for global expansion. As the account base broadened outside the U.S., he soon realized the enormity of the shipping and managing task ahead and that continued direct sales to the ink manufacturers offered the best prospect as far as control was concerned. Pantone would license and ship in bulk to the foreign ink manufacturers who would then distribute or sell the product to printers. The new strategy that Rudy discussed with Larry would require that Larry travel to Europe two to three times a year while he continued to sell to the South American market.

"Nobody can sell this product like you can, Larry. Since you invented it, you're the best person to explain it and get distributors on board. It's the only way to go."

Rudy's logic convinced Larry, who wasted no time launching the plan. Larry selected dozens of prospects from among the clients he had sourced through referrals and through the international printing manufacturers' directory. Charting his destinations on the map, he chose dates for each stop. Next, he sat down and penned an introductory letter to each potential client to explain the purpose of his visit and ask for an appointment to "discuss this great idea that I've got going in the United States." With the new Pantone making news since 1964, Larry figured that they must have had some knowledge of the system — or at least had heard of it. All he had to do was hint at how it could help them.

Much-needed sales eventually added even more pressure. Larry's inventories rose while sales stagnated. Ink manufacturers, who had purchased books all along since 1963, had not received new requests for books from their end-users, the printers and designers. The number of color options had not increased, and they just weren't wearing them out. So new books didn't seem necessary.

By early fall 1968, once the meetings had been scheduled, Larry purchased an around-the-world airline ticket. Had Braniff International flown cross-Pacific or -Atlantic, Larry might have been tempted to fly the airline known for its vividly painted planes of lemon, beige, ocher, turquoise, orange, light and dark blue colors, popular at the onset of the Age of Aquarius. But "TWA had a great deal going — $1200 for a first class ticket," recalls Larry. "And as long as I didn't double back, I could keep going west until I got back to New York." The international adventure about to begin, Larry also packed for stops in the U.S., including Washington, D.C., Detroit, Chicago, Denver, Los Angeles, San Francisco (plastered with innumerable, fixating, psychedelic DayGlo and black light concert posters), and finally, Anchorage. From there, he crossed the Pacific into Asia, visiting Tokyo and Osaka in Japan (where their color preferences remained lighter and somewhat restrained, with white being the favorite), Hong Kong, Bangkok and Ceylon (Sri Lanka). He continued to Tel Aviv and Europe, where he stopped in Rome, Frankfurt (known for its partiality to darker, more somber colors), Paris, Amsterdam and London. At each meeting during the month-long trip, he pitched his product and its benefits to their businesses and to their industry.

Though Larry spoke no languages other than English, color communication, the common denominator, appeared to break all barriers. With the help of interpreters, Larry struck deals one after another.

In Japan, though, Larry faced a dilemma far greater than language. The two principal ink manufacturers — Dainippon Ink and Toyo — proved an almost insurmountable problem. Not only did they maintain their own color books, they controlled up to 75 percent of the market by helping printers finance their equipment with the proviso that they buy ink from one of their companies. An illegal practice in the U.S., in Japan the manufacturers' market grip only tightened as Pantone moved in.

While the Japanese ink monopoly looked at Pantone as a threat, the less sizeable manufacturers regarded Pantone and its 500-color palette as a means to elevate their status and expand their businesses. In both Tokyo and Osaka, these smaller manufacturers surprised Larry with a mass gathering to hear him speak rather than sitting with him one-on-one. There, he stood before a sea of unfamiliar faces to extol the virtues of his product. With the room perfectly quiet, and all eyes fixed on him, he cleared his throat and began to speak. Then the interpreter did the same.

When he finished speaking, no one clapped. Instead, the audience began to buzz among themselves. Larry stood equally silent. He was sure he had asked for the sale. Had he offended his audience in some way? Uncomfortable now, he remained unsure of what was happening, until one man stood to speak for the group. In fractured English he said, "Mr. Herbert, we are please to be part of Pantone. We will sign." Then everyone applauded.

The two hold-outs, Dainippon Ink and Toyo, took several more years to become licensed to use the PANTONE MATCHING SYSTEM. Ultimately, they were forced to acquiesce by designers and art directors who used their ink, but who also relied on the Pantone chips for matching. The two Japanese mega-companies had to adapt to stay alive.

After his final stay in London, Larry happily boarded his flight to return to New York and his office where he joked with his staff, "I lost fifteen pounds on that trip, and it wasn't in English money."

Expanding the Empire

Larry's success stemmed not only from his product but also from his remarkable timing. As no clearly defined color system existed at this time — at least no international system in the graphic arts market. While color books and cards were available in Germany and London, they amounted to no more than copycat industries, with palette selections of a mere sixty or seventy colors. Surprising, since Europe had always been marked as fashionista central where palettes were first determined.

Still, that Larry offered a greater color choice was not the only factor having an impact on these sales. The genius, of course, in Larry's plan, was the fairness factor: all players on the same field. Reasonable terms gave all the manufacturers an even chance. And, not only would the manufacturer's name grace the cover, one could order as few as 50 books. Larry understood that while a few customers were inclined to order the minimum number of books, most would want to blanket their customer base.

Just as he had done in the U.S., Larry traveled armed with a list of pigment suppliers with whom he worked. Many of these resources came from international companies; others shipped internationally from the United States. Japan, of course, locked out suppliers other than their own, so there Larry did the smart thing and listed only Japanese suppliers as a resource. Mostly, though, he easily forged direct relationships around the world. Without middlemen, Pantone held closer control of color, income, and lessened the possibility of piracy.

THE KING *of* COLOR

8

Pirates in Inky Waters: Protecting the PANTONE® Mark

Larry had taken steps to protect his product and name before embarking on his whirlwind trip in 1968. He applied for and secured trademarks in a number of countries assuming this would lessen the likelihood of infringement. Yet with all this forethought and planning, he returned home from his travels to discover those very problems: first, a Brazilian customer had registered the PANTONE Name and used it as its own; and second, Para-Tone, Inc., a Chicago-based art supply distributor, had pirated his system for artist materials.

The Brazilian customer, an ink manufacturer, when questioned, used the excuse that it was protecting the name on Pantone's behalf. Larry's reply: he was capable of handling the issue for himself and requested that they simply transfer the registered name to him. Their answer, "Well, no, we think we'll keep it," led to unexpected legal wrangling.

105

A company's name is an identifying factor, one reason why a company like McDonald's, for example, willingly institutes lawsuits against anyone who uses the "Mc" as part of their own name. A trademark generally comprises one or a combination of the following elements: name, word, phrase, logo, symbol, design, image, even color. Such is the case with McDonald's yellow arches, or the distinctive yellow and black Kodak film box, or the striped yellow and black design element of Cliff Notes. Where color alone is concerned, when it is an integral part of the product's identity, as in the case of Owens-Corning pink fiberglass insulation, color may be included as an element of the trademark, thus, in this example, excluding other insulation manufacturers from using it. In Pantone's case, the company had to prove that its name had appeared in Brazil *before* the unauthorized registration took place. It had, allowing Larry to secure the Brazilian trademark.

The situation regarding Para-Tone, Inc. constituted outright piracy as well as conspiracy. Pantone had created a line of colored papers and acetates, for use by artists and designers, to match the color system. Realizing the financial potential of such a venture, Para-Tone began to distribute a line of papers and acetates as well. The problem: Para-Tone marketed Pantone's exact system under its name rather than Pantone's. They even went so far as to offer their dealers a Para-Tone/Pantone cross-reference guide that read, "PMS 123 is our 123"— an admission to copying if ever there was one.

Trying to resolve the situation on its own, Pantone attempted to negotiate a licensing agreement with Para-Tone, but they refused to acknowledge the issue.

To add further insult to injury, the Glenn-Killian Ink Company, one of the largest and oldest ink manufacturers in the U.S., who had sold the copyright to its *Formulator* system to Para-Tone, decided to counter for what they considered infringement of the Glenn-Killian System as the basis of the PANTONE MATCHING SYSTEM.

To Larry, this blow seemed yet another example of a company trying to take Pantone down. As a kid who learned to stick up for himself on the streets of Brooklyn, Larry would come out fighting when backed into a corner. With this indignation, Larry saw red and set out on the attack. He knew that, beyond a doubt, he would have to prove that the two systems differed.

Larry had never regarded the Glenn-Killian system worthy of consideration, much less copying. He was familiar with and had worked with all the systems offered by the ink manufacturers — Glenn-Killian, Lewis Roberts, and Inmont — but had never felt that any stood alone as complete or logical or that any would stand up as building blocks for a more expansive system.

During the direct examination, the man who originated the Glenn-Killian *Formulator* revealed that the basic building blocks of the Pantone System were so entirely different that Para-Tone, the defendant, couldn't actually claim that Larry had copied any of the colors.

Then Pantone's attorney responded with, "You really want to hurt

Mr. Herbert, don't you?"

"Objection, your honor!"

"Overruled. Answer the question."

"Well yeah, he affected my business to a degree, because he came out with a different book."

Nevertheless, the case dragged on for several years following its inception in 1968 and, in 1971, subsequently shifted venues from the New York courts to the U.S. Court in Chicago. Larry, of course, made the trip. As he entered the courtroom, marveling at the courtroom walls plastered with pictures of Abraham Lincoln, he worried about the judge he would be dealing with after what seemed like endless hearings in front of the federal judges in New York: first Judge James Mansfield, who had also presided over a case for the Wallpaper Council and understood color and copyright infringement; then Judge Milton Pollack, who, instead of entering a decision, had sent the case to Chicago.

As proceedings began, he immediately felt the calming demeanor of presiding Judge Abraham Lincoln Marovitz. But he couldn't suppress a chuckle when Judge Marovitz, wearing a black velvet smoking jacket, gold embellished velvet slippers and smoking a cigarette with what could have been an ostentatious, Hollywood-esque, tortoise-tone cigarette holder if not for its stubbiness, invited the opposing parties into his chambers in an attempt to settle what had proven a difficult and tenuous situation.

Inside his richly stained, walnut-paneled chambers, Marovitz first queried the owner of Para-Tone, Myra Woods.

"Why do you feel you have the use of Pantone's colors?"

"Colors are free," she replied. "And PANTONE Colors should be free for everybody to use. It's a matter of principle, Your Honor."

The judge then asked, "How do you spell that, "p-a-l" or "p-l-e"?" Myra Woods didn't reply, so Marovitz continued, "I guess that means we are going to court." He requested that both parties prepare for trial and ended the meeting.

At trial, Larry took the stand first. During the next forty-five minutes, he discussed the PANTONE System and his methodical research: the length of time required for its development, its originality, and the steps he had taken to ensure that no one else's work had been infringed upon. During cross-examination, Para-Tone's attorney produced a document, a letter written by Larry, in which Larry had stated that an entire group of ink manufacturers backed the system. This referenced document confused Larry. He actually couldn't remember it, until the yellow-marked passage was placed before him.

The Para-Tone attorney pressed on, "Well, Mr. Herbert, was this statement true?"

"This was a promotional letter. Commercial puffery. It's a stretch of the truth," replied Larry.

Immediately following Larry's testimony and cross-examination, Judge Marovitz slowly brushed his palms across his thinning gray hair, not so much to straighten it as to give notice that he was about to speak. Announcing that he was suspending for the day, he requested a hot copy of the day's transcript. The next morning at 10:00 a.m., he turned to the Pantone team, looked over his Ben Franklin specs and asked, `You don't have any more witnesses, do you?"

Larry understood the rhetorical nature of the question. He had seen Marovitz in action while in chambers. But Larry wasn't ready to end it there. He had lined up a healthy list of other witnesses to testify on his behalf. Marovitz, however, declined, commenting that he really didn't need to hear from any further Pantone witnesses.

"I'd actually like to hear from Para-Tone's color matcher," the Judge specified.

Once the Judge began his questioning, the outcome became abundantly clear to Larry.

"During Mr. Herbert's testimony, he states that the building blocks between his system and the Glenn-Killian system are entirely different. Now, Mr. Smith, when you mixed the colors for the Para-Tone system, where did you get your colors from?" asked the Judge. Then, lowering his voice, "Remember, you are under oath."

"Well, I matched them to the PANTONE MATCHING SYSTEM," replied Smith.

Point, set and match.

The day before pronouncement of judgment, Larry flew back to Chicago. That night, Marovitz's clerk requested six copies of the Findings of Fact and Conclusions of Law drawn up by Larry's legal team. On July 18, 1971, the judge began his remarks. This case had wasted the court's time, he pointed out. Then, much to the surprise of the Pantone team, he granted Pantone everything requested in their Findings.

"We entered a lot of stuff into the decision we thought the judge might throw out," recalls Larry. "But he didn't throw out anything."

For Larry, this coup carried a bonus: he could avert any pending infringement cases by simply handing over the carefully crafted Decision. Companies like Crawford Ink, with its Mix-and-Match system, would now run the other way. Pantone's right to its system, trademark and copyright, now tested in court, became a landmark decision that would continue to be tested through the years.

Despite his hands-down victory, Larry refused to press further for damages. Though Para-Tone had made money from the sales of its products based on his system, Larry no longer wanted to spend inordinate amounts of time and money pushing forward for what could potentially be a paltry settlement. To control potential problems down the line and protect his business, Larry had fought the good fight.

Legal battles like these drained the company financially and taxed him personally. With no time left for a personal life, his every waking, breathing hour dedicated to the founding and leading of the company into the future, everything else was pushed into the background and everyone else became second-class citizens. Roberta's agitation pushed Larry further adrift. Still, he had no choice but to protect his business interests. The results more than justified the cost.

Winning this particular case helped secure one of Pantone's largest contracts of that time. The blue chip corporation 3M had caught wind of the energetic little company "that could" when Pantone gained tremendous ground in the U.S. and began to make its mark in Europe. In 1968, 3M had approached Pantone to create a series of color-proofing sheets for its Printing Products Division that tied into the PANTONE Numbering System, but reflected the most popular 3M colors. At that point, 3M had not offered any sort of working identification code on their sheets and viewed the PANTONE System as an important advancement. This royalty-based license, called the 3M Color-Key system, would also bear the PANTONE Trademark.

As the Para-Tone case went to trial, however, 3M could not jeopardize the project or its name. 3M needed assurances that it would, in fact, be working with the valid system owner, and postponed the deal while the trademark issue was being tried. This was a blow to Larry. He wanted, no, needed their business. The Pantone coffers lay near bankruptcy and required the money infusion more than ever. Hog-tied by the Para-Tone case for three years, Larry had anxiously waited to finalize this deal. When the verdict was handed down, he ran to the nearest phone and called his 3M contact to put the deal to bed. He gave 3M the news.

"We already know," remarked the voice on the other end.

"How could you know?" asked Larry. "It just happened."

"We had someone sitting in court watching the proceedings."

Papers were signed shortly thereafter. Larry's small company, making barely $1 million a year, now held 3M in its pocket. David had met and tamed his Goliath. But other battles waged on.

Back in New York, Larry eagerly delivered the court decision to several other companies with whom he was legally embroiled. The cases were dropped.

He felt vindicated. After years of struggle against plagiarists and pirates, he also felt in control. One might even say safe.

For Larry, juggling nonsense lawsuits had become business as usual. While Pantone rebounded, Sinclair and Valentine — the ink manufacturer with whom Pantone had had a precarious working relationship for many years — began to offer its own color codes on its ink cans. Just as Pantone had prefixed its numeric codes with the acronym PMS, Sinclair & Valentine assigned its codes with an S&V symbol. The problem: Sinclair and Valentine had appropriated Pantone's copyrighted numbering system. When Larry received word of the infringement, he purchased the S&V product line, had it tested and discovered that every color was a dead on match to Pantone's own. How long had this been going on, wondered Larry?

Larry first approached the president of the company, Howard Soriano, who, though refusing to own up to any wrongdoing on his part, wanted Larry to supply him with an agreement stipulating that S&V would not use the PANTONE System. Larry stood dumbfounded by Soriano's twisted idea. What chutzpah!

"I don't have to give you an agreement," insisted Larry. "Just don't use it and that would be that."

Soriano stubbornly held his ground. "No, I want an agreement that says I won't use it."

These useless dialogues led Larry to seek out Jim Renson, vice president of marketing, and show him the proof. It didn't take long for the S&V President to be fired not only for the infringement but also for inciting others to drop the PANTONE System.

When the dust settled, Jim Renson called Larry.

"Herbert, I'd like to see you in my office 9:00 a.in. Monday morning in Englewood Cliffs."

"I'll be there," Larry replied. He had wanted their business from the start.

Larry pulled up to the building and entered Renson's office at 9:07 a.m.

"Herbert, I said nine o'clock," the marketing vice president barked. "You're seven minutes late."

"I'm seven minutes late, but you guys are seven years late," Larry replied with a chuckle. "Let's get to work and get you up to speed." Thus began a lasting relationship.

Pantone's legal woes, however, continued. At the same time, he began his legal squabble with Para-Tone, an unscrupulous PANTONE Distributor, Mico-Type, was discovered selling PANTONE Books and color sheets in its own discount retail venues at drastically discounted prices, undercutting the independent stores. The independents complained to Larry, but he felt that his hands were tied, until, that is, Mico-Type broke their contract by missing a payment due date. The agreement with Mico-Type specified a purchase quantity and payment by year-end. So when they placed their order December 31st but didn't pay for it, Larry sent a letter canceling the contract. Mico-Type instituted a lawsuit against Pantone only to lose the case — the firm clearly had not held up its end of the arrangement.

Putting out wildfires, while one of Larry's strengths, brought Pantone to the edge of survival. Each crusade diminished the company's profits, prompting Larry to consider a crucial change in 1970. This latest costly legal battle, though an indisputable victory for Pantone, brought Larry to an important decision. He would take Pantone public for an infusion of much needed cash.

In April 1970, Larry offered 100,000 Regulation A shares at $3.00 per share for Pantone. Over the next few years, during the mini boom experienced in 1972 and 1973, the shares rose to $7.00, and then slowly relinquished their gain. The problem, as Larry saw it, was that the stock market did not understand Pantone's business. Investors understood the manufacture of commodities, objects you could hold or touch, but selling color eluded them. As Larry's mother used to say to him, 'You're in the color business? And from this you make a living?"

In 1972, under the watchful eyes of his Board of Directors and stockholders, Larry decided that the best way to make money was not to spend it. Licensing Pantone's products — in this case, the matching papers, acetates and markers the company had produced since 1964 and that had infiltrated the worldwide market — marked an important business step in the future of Pantone. Securing the arrangement, though, proved another test of wills for Larry.

Shortly after Larry embarked on his new plan, Letraset, a company out of England with very similar products and a much larger distribution, caught wind of the aggressive little company that had charged full steam into their turf. They approached Larry about buying Pantone. "I turned them down," explained Larry, matter-of-factly. "But we eventually agreed to give them exclusive manufacturing and distribution rights for the world. It was a complicated agreement that we actually finalized on a QE2 trip from Cherbourg to New York." Over the next 20 years, Letraset, eventually acquired by Esselte, would pay Pantone millions of dollars in royalties and for its products. By 1977, Larry had had enough bending to the will of stockholders who had more questions than Larry had time to answer and still get work done. When the stock slipped to $.60 a share, Larry decided to buy back his company. Economically, the timing could not have been worse. The tedium of answering to investors and not being able to spend enough time growing the business as a result had taken its toll on both owner and company, contributing to sluggish dynamics, unchanged products and stagnant sales. Larry paid his investors $1.00 a share and vowed never to relinquish control of Pantone again — at least not to anyone who did not carry Herbert as a last name. He once again turned to the business of growing Pantone instead of explaining it or justifying it.

Fully in charge now, newly motivated, and ready to strike out, Larry moved to reposition Pantone. Promoting Pantone as a dominant color language proved Herculean, but challenge fueled Larry. He faced the unknown head-on — in all but one instance, that is.

THE KING *of* COLOR

9

The Empire Strikes Back

Between the years 1974 and 1977, while in the midst of rescuing Pantone from copycats, thieves and conspirators, Larry and his executive team traveled extensively to Europe and Asia, gaining recognition for the Pantone name. In January 1977, just before the annual DRUPA (the German acronym for 'druck und papier,' meaning printing and paper) Show in Dusseldorf, Pantone prepared for a major market penetration of its PANTONE Color Data System in West Germany and other parts of Europe. Larry had earmarked over $150,000 in advertising for two important European exhibitions, Frankfurt in March and Dusseldorf in June. Prior to the first show in Frankfurt, he scheduled crucial business meetings in Siegburg, Munich, Frankfurt, Cologne, Hanover and Paris, accompanied by two of his Pantone executives, Rainer Sigel and Norbert Klein. After his meeting with France-Couleurs in Paris and before the show in Frankfurt, Larry and crew had one last conference with Pantone's public relations firm in Cologne, West Germany. Knowing that this next day would involve lots of discussion and schmoozing, Larry boarded his flight at Frankfurt Airport, planning to take a cab to the hotel in Cologne and get a good night's rest.

He stepped off Lufthansa flight 129 in Cologne (KÖLN) that night and approached Passport Control. Everything occurred as it had many times before: a dark green-uniformed officer looked over his passport and handed it back without a word. Larry replaced his passport inside his jacket pocket and walked the narrow hallway to the exit. Klein and Sigel lagged behind. Suddenly, two machine-gun-armed officers blocked him.

"Halt," they ordered, their palms raised to his face.

A third officer from the Passport Control booth joined them, demanding Larry's passport. This had never happened before, so Larry couldn't imagine any problem and willingly acquiesced to all commands.

"You will come with us," demanded the first officer.

Saliva flooded Larry's throat. He swallowed hard.

"Why? Where are you taking me? I haven't done anything. What's going on?" The questions rushed out.

Silence.

Larry's head began to spin. He froze on the spot as his executives Sigel and Klein came up behind him. Sigel spoke fluent German and questioned the officer.

"You're under arrest!" he reported incredulously to an even more astonished Larry.

As the police separated Klein and Sigel from Larry, Norbert Klein hollered, "They are serious, Larry. You've got to think what this might be. A hotel bill? Think. Anything here in Cologne?"

An incident flashed through his mind. "Hertz! 1974," he cried over his shoulder. On a business trip in 1974, accompanied by his brother-in-law, Mike Garin, Larry had returned his rental car at the small Port St. Cloud Hertz office in Paris. They arrived late in the evening and handed the car over to the only person manning the station — a mechanic.

"We have papers to show it was taken care of," Larry cried before armed officers whisked him away to a small, spare room underground, ordered him to remove his clothing and searched him.

Again, silence met his questions.

Finally, he was told that they didn't know why he was being detained but that his name and passport number had come up in the computer — HERBERT, LAWRENCE, 012429 DETAIN.

"Is this because of a simple rental car snafu?" Larry asked. "We have proof. Maybe you've mistaken me for someone else."

Yes, of course that had to be it. Since the Munich Olympics tragedy in 1972, security had tightened to a pinhole.

"No more talking," the guard shot back without looking up.

Norbert Klein found his way downstairs. Larry could hear him utter the words "American Consulate," and the Passport Control Officer countering with "Cologne Prison."

Nausea welled up. Larry could not believe what he heard. He, an affluent American, Gestapo-ed to a German prison.

Did his being Jewish have anything to do with the arrest? In his panicked state, he assumed the worst.

It wouldn't have been the first time that he'd been confronted with anti-Semitism. As early as 1966, when big manufacturing companies had actively moved to sink Pantone, IPI (which became Inmont) had a vice president of marketing who hated Larry. This vice president had devised a color book that flopped, so Larry took the opportunity to speak to the man's boss and the marketing director about the PANTONE System. They agreed there was value to be had and indicated they would get back to him after some internal discussion. At the meeting, just as they had come to a decision to sign up with Pantone, the aforementioned vice president of marketing rose up in his chair and blurted, "If you buy these books, you're going to make this Jew richer than he already is."

This time, however, Larry was in Germany and about to be imprisoned for a nameless crime. His legs wobbled and his stomach churned. Thoughts of the Holocaust flooded through him. He let out a huge sigh as he recalled Elsie Williamson's words, "I am ashamed of what my people did…" He hoped her countrymen felt the same. The gates of Cologne Prison swallowed the transport van into the belly of the courtyard. Night had fallen and the dampness clung like smoke from a cheap cigar. Surrounded by four-story walls, barely a light was visible through window blocks darkened by years of grime. Armed guards deposited Larry at 'reception.' An older, red-faced, jowl-necked man, barely stuffed into his uniform, looked up at Larry.

"Who did you kill?" he asked in a thick German accent.

"No one. I didn't kill anyone," replied Larry. "Why am I here?"

"Then how much did you steal? You must know how much you stole."

As often as Larry denied charges and demanded answers, he was bombarded with more questions and accusations. An unshakable surrealness surrounded him. And he still knew nothing.

Strip-searched a second humiliating time, he was relieved of his belongings, escorted into a utility room to retrieve his own blanket, marched to a steel-doored cell and motioned in. When he couldn't move his feet, the guard shoved him. The six- by ten-foot room somehow diminished him. This proud man, who had built a company on an idea, stood powerless…in a prison cell…in Germany. He looked up to see a row of dirt-laden window blocks and a low wattage bulb. He was thankful for the light.

It was past 10 p.m. A narrow wooden slab dangled from wall chains. A toilet, well used and with the stench to prove it, sat in the corner. Disbelief turned to fear. Larry folded his blanket to use as a cushion and sat on the slab. He had to remain calm, organize his thoughts. It was Friday. Back home, rush hour would start soon. Before he could adjust to his surroundings, the light went out. He was alone. In the dark, his heart pounded.

As Larry sat isolated and scared in his jail cell, his team scrambled to straighten things out. Told by the detective that Larry had been transferred, charged and was not allowed visitors, Norbert Klein and Rainer Sigel immediately headed for the Central Railway station to place a call to the Pantone offices in Moonachie, New Jersey. The Haupt Bahnkof main station, open 24 hours a day, provided a bank of phone booths for international calls at a reasonable price. Assigned a booth, they waited for someone to answer on the other side of the world. As they explained the incident to Jack Siderman, Pantone's vice president of marketing, the two agreed that the Hertz rental car incident Larry had alluded to, which dated back to 1974, could be the only answer. They simply needed the files as proof.

Jack immediately called Mike Garin into his office, the only other person in the Mercedes when it was returned. Mike was family in two ways. Not only was he Larry's brother-in-law, he had been with Pantone since the inception of the PANTONE MATCHING SYSTEM and was an integral part of its growth.

Mike Garin and Jack Siderman instantly realized that they would require the aid of Joyce Schwartz — Larry's secretary for ten years and Pantone's unofficial motherly shoulder to cry on — to find the papers. But she had already left for the weekend.

They left a message at Joyce's home, then immediately called Pantone's corporate counsel, Lawson Bernstein, at his home. Since he felt this had all the markings of an international incident, he, in turn, called New York Senator Jacob Javits's office, hoping someone would still be there. Meanwhile, Siderman and Garin began their search for the papers while continuing to ring Joyce Schwartz's home.

With the workweek's clock ticking down, Mike Garin frantically called the Hertz offices in Manhattan.

He introduced himself and then explained, "We are in the midst of a legal problem. They're holding the president of our company in Germany, and we need a copy of the papers that prove the case against Mr. Herbert was dropped."

"I'm sorry," reported the voice on the other end. "There's no one here who can help you. Everyone has left for the weekend."

Mike, an immensely shy man in person, but whom Larry considered an extremely capable executive — a thinking man and a man of action — called Hertz in Los Angeles, where it was still mid-afternoon.

It took some convincing and several 'hold' times, but he pried loose the name of the Hertz executive, Gerhard Meier, involved in the 1974 incident, as well as the name of the executive now in charge of operations in Germany. The information was passed on to Norbert Klein, now entrenched at a Holiday Inn near the prison.

In the meantime, Joyce Schwartz had by chance stopped home on her way out for the evening and received the frantic messages. Calling in without delay, she explained that the files were in the attic Space.

The retrieved Hertz documents had to be transported to Kennedy Airport and received by 8:00 p.in. to make the 9:00 p.in. Lufthansa courier pouch. Mike arranged for a helicopter from Newark Airport to Kennedy Airport, but the twelve-mile drive to

Newark from Moonachie could prove even more difficult during the Friday rush hour.

Ignorant of all these efforts, Larry sat in his darkened cell with only the green luminescence[19] of his watch dial to comfort him. In his heart, he knew that Sigel and Klein were out there working hard to resolve the problem, but every hour that passed left him feeling more distraught. He began to weep.

The ghostly past chilled Larry's bones as he pulled the blanket from beneath him to wrap around his shoulders. The uncontrollable pounding of his heart marked the dead air. A soft, relentless swilling took over. Dogs barked outside his window. Carts clanked over cobblestones. Trucks rumbled by, whispering the wounded cries of condemned Jews. Only yellow stars appeared in the black abyss. He was losing control of his senses.

By midnight, Sigel and Klein still had not secured German counsel for Larry. They thumbed through the phone book, A through Z, noting individual professions listed with home numbers. One after another, they were turned away: It was the dead of night and the plight of a jailed American disinterested them - until they reached Herr Mueller of the firm, Mueller and Mueller. The son of an established criminal lawyer in Cologne, Mueller had connections and could move swiftly.

Sometime after 8:00 a.m. the next morning, Mueller met with

---

[19] *Phosphorescent inks absorb light, store it and slowly and continuously radiate it back. Unlike fluorescent inks, which only radiate in ultraviolet light, phosphorescent ink continues to glow in total darkness.*

Larry for the first time. He concluded that although the matter of the missing Hertz car had been resolved years ago, the warrant issued at that time had not been withdrawn. Larry sat in a prison cell because of someone's ineptness. And it was Saturday.

Though it was a weekend, Rainer Sigel managed to contact an old friend, an esteemed attorney in Frankfurt coincidentally named Hans Herbert. Herbert located Gerhard Meier, the head of Hertz Frankfurt. By 11 a.m., he had gathered the appropriate documentation, witnesses and evidence to present to a judge at police headquarters. Hans Herbert pressed his case in Frankfurt while, in Cologne, Larry was brought to interrogation once again, asked to sign a confession (which he refused), photographed with a numbered hang tag around his neck, and booked like a criminal!

Suddenly, they handed Larry his belongings. *They've cleared up this whole misunderstanding,* Larry thought jubilantly. *I'm going to be released.*

Instead, the prosecutor informed Larry that he would be transferred to yet another prison. The forty-seven-year-old couldn't catch his breath. Slack-jawed and glazed over, Larry could never have imagined this. Just then, the hum of the Telex caught everyone's attention and spewed forth the words, *Lawrence Herbert: all charges dropped. Release at once.*

Still dazed, Larry only heard the guttural sounds of German as he tried to make sense of the commotion around him.

Norbert Klein and Herr Mueller ran down the corridor to greet

Larry and confirm the news. The threesome would await the judge's final signature of release together. Mueller suggested that Larry and company leave Germany as quickly as possible, since the informational system would still carry his name. Larry gladly obliged.

On board his flight, the attendant offered Larry a glass of champagne. He accepted and quipped, "Leave the bottle, won't you?" The bedraggled, pale man finally found comfort and fell asleep.

Within a few days of his return, the entire office had found out about the incident. Even though some tried to maintain a sense of cheerfulness, Larry's comeback revealed his fright. "It's not funny. It's just not funny," he blurted with slumped shoulders.

In all the years Larry spent promoting Pantone as the dominant color language, he had had his share of problems. Lawsuits and enemies came with the territory, but this experience would haunt him. Still, Larry was not a man to let the personal get in the way of business. As the saying goes, however, life happens while we are busy making other plans.

10

When Life Hands You Lemons

As the 1960s waned, radical youth, political liberalism, intellectualism and social confusion gave way to a more conservative value construct. Richard Nixon took office as the thirty-seventh President, and as the Vietnam War split the nation, the youth of America raged on, culminating in the Kent State Massacre in 1970. In the meantime, America landed a man on the moon. Middle Americans, now half the population, began reclaiming their way of life, balancing the threats of student dissension and black militarism. *TIME* magazine portrayed this complex group of Middle Americans as 'The Man and Woman of The Year.'

Businesses had embraced the youth movement, its freedom and colorfulness. Though conflict surrounded America, it also wrapped itself in a robe of bright, electric colors. Pantone had helped see to that. Since the inception of the PANTONE MATCHING SYSTEM, the company had continued to develop its product line while continuing to work with corporations like RCA (red), Howard Johnson (orange), and Eastern Airlines (blue) to standardize and formulate their colors. Pantone launched its first PMS Artist Materials in 1965, and in 1968, offered the first four-color Process Guide, extending color possibilities to some 15,000 tints, shades and screens. Pantone also made available a Color Tint Selector for the design field.

As businesses and advertisers demanded newer colors to accent their Flower Power and Age of Aquarius selling themes, Larry forged a license with DayGlo to produce fluorescent-based colors. Adding to his artists' materials, he provided self-stick transparent color/tint overlay films in a palette of 424 colors and effects.

During the latter part of the 1960s, the nation, as a whole, pushed through divisive social issues while businesses, like construction, seemingly pressed on unimpeded. Inflation and unemployment had remained low since the early 1960s; the Consumer Price Index — what a dollar could buy — increased only slightly each year.

Change wafted foully through the air as the decade turned. Fashion trends abruptly changed, forcing hemlines from mid-thigh to mid-calf, raising a furor among women. The once intensely-colored rainbow faded under the return to a so-called more sophisticated look, which presented Depression era colors with updated names like basic black, raisin deep-red, brandied coffee and ripe plum. American women tried to put on a colorful face with what Estee Lauder Inc. described as "the return to real makeup," thus subjugating the natural look of the late 60s.

Retail skulked along as consumer spending declined: the 1970

Christmas season was all but jolly. By August 1971, Nixon sought to strengthen the dollar by freezing wages, salaries, rents and prices for a ninety-day period. Food prices, including packaged goods, farm produce and especially red meat, hit unreasonably high prices, sending senior citizens to the cat food aisle. Non-food items, such as newsprint, became scarce. Interest rates soared and Nixon once again froze prices in June 1973. Economists deemed that this action occurred "90 percent too late."[20] With production of goods plummeting, layoffs spread like wildfire. The Arab oil embargo created an energy crisis unseen for a generation.

Under the threat of impeachment for his role in the Watergate scandal, Nixon resigned office on August 8, 1974, leaving Gerald Ford to head a broken country. Inflation high-jumped into the double digits in 1974, and the confidence of the American public hit an all-time low, plummeting 30 percent during September and October alone.

Fear and panic ensued. Businesses suffered, Pantone among them. Within a decade, Larry had managed to restructure Pantone from a small-time press which printed custom color charts for ink manufacturers to one known for its ability to match and create colors for clients. He penetrated and developed previously untapped territories to expand sales. He recognized that this would keep him even busier juggling every aspect of the business, including protecting turf already carved out. What he could not foresee, though, was the

---

[20] *Robert Nathan, a member Of TIMES's Board of Economists as quoted in Time Magazine in the article The Gut Issue: Prices Running Amuck, TIME Magazine, August 27, 1973.*

THE KING *of* COLOR

HOW DOES YOUR DAY-GLO?

Although we associate those eye-popping DayGlo colors with the 1960s counter culture revolution, LSD and Flower Power, the uniquely bright substance, created from natural fluorescent minerals, came about through an act of fate paired with genius. While attending the College of Chemistry at the University of California in the early 1930s, Bob Switzer worked unloading crates for Safeway Supermarket stores at their rail yard. One day he tripped, hit his head and fed into a coma. He regained consciousness a few months later to discover that his vision had been permanently impaired, ending his chances of becoming a doctor. At home recovering, he was subjected to a darkened room. To pass the hours of dreary boredom, he began waving fluorescent minerals in the air and watched their glow. Once up on his feet, he decided to experiment by mixing the minerals with varnish. Before long, the amateur magician and chemistry student brewed a stable emulsion, which he and his brother Joe referred to as Day-Glo, and used to create standing stage tricks in the dark.

The U.S. Army caught wind of the products remarkable stage success and commissioned Switzer to incorporate his pigments into fabric for the North African troops, who were falling victim to friendly fire from Allied aircraft. Thus began the high visibility careers of Joe and Bob Switzer in 1946, which can be seen on supermarket shelves and children's toys, attention grabbing signals to hunting clothes, rock posters to fashion. Colors with added fluorescence are 75 percent more visible.

When Bob Switzer died in 1997, CBS television acknowledged him in an obituary: "Thank you, Robert Switzer, for DayGlo. The world is brighter now, since you came along. Even in the dark." A neon yellow golf ball was placed beside harm as he was laid to rest.

family invasion that would impact his march toward color domination.

For years, when not traveling, Larry had taken his three kids, born at two-year intervals, to work with him on their days off from school. Richard recalls his father's office at 461 Eighth Avenue in New York, as he watched Madison Square Garden IV become the new venue for the NY Knicks' games that the two would later attend together. As youngsters, the Herbert children would sit for hours in Larry's office and draw with markers and paper that were keyed to the PANTONE System.

The Herbert children had been born into color and had grown up understanding what Pantone stood for. Not surprisingly, they would all end up working in their father's company. Not one, however, had asked their father for a job. Still, starting in 1974, they acquired summer positions.

"What are you doing here?" he queried his eldest, Lisa

"Oh, we just called Joe in the warehouse and asked if we could get jobs for the summer," Lisa replied.

Each child performed the minor tasks assigned to them, working their way up to shrink-wrapping, attaching screw posts in the bindery and eventually learning quality control on the latest color-measuring spectrophotometric equipment in the laboratory. Over the summers, they learned various aspects of the business into which they had been born.

As a result, each would evolve within the company, create a niche and prove an asset. But it wouldn't be the smoothest of rides, since as Larry put it, "I never *hired* them. One summer day as I walked through the bindery, there they were, putting together books."

Despite their involvement in his company, Larry's relationship with his children had become somewhat strained. In 1972, after years of growing discord over Larry's heavy travel schedule and an unwillingness to be flexible on Roberta's part, Larry had separated from his wife and moved into New York City, where he stayed during the week. Though he would return home to spend the weekends with his children, the transition proved difficult. Larry's work-burdened days drifted into lonely nights. He missed his home and family life. But he. Felt drained and felt that the bickering strained everyone.

Richard's Bar Mitzvah in 1974, a blessing for Larry, also marked him with a heavy heart. He would now make the change to New York permanent. However, before doing so, he consulted a child psychologist. The kids were still impressionable, and the idea of their parents no longer together could release a myriad of feelings. He did not want them to feel abandoned.

As the three Herbert children occupied themselves with school, friends and their summer jobs at Pantone, and as Larry dove into his newfound swinging bachelorhood in New York, he managed — insisted on — maintaining a standing Tuesday night dinner date with his children. Yet, with all his resoluteness, the three somehow couldn't always synchronize their schedules to keep their date with him.

No one, and certainly not Larry, could have predicted that the

Herbert children would eventually head Pantone and turn it into a family business. Not until, that is, one by one they arrived at Pantone's doorstep to take permanent positions.

Following his stint inside the German prison, he had wished his children had been present, working at the company instead of in school, to comfort him. Yet even if they had been there, he couldn't have turned to them. Even now, he couldn't turn to anyone for help. Traumatized, the experience unexpectedly crept into his personal and working relationships that entire year. He found himself unable to sleep, afraid both of the dark and of sleep itself. When he did eventually drift off each night, he would regularly wake up in mid-nightmare and spend the remaining hours until morning pacing the floors. Unable to shake his sense of distress, his drinking escalated. Though surrounded by friends, Larry's 48th birthday party, planned by Lisa shortly after the incident, brought him no comfort or joy. Lisa remarked afterward that he looked like a "zombie with a smile."

Depression and moodiness overcame him and pervaded the office where he appeared at whim, snapping and barking at workers. Even to loyal workers and friends like Mike Garin, he spewed like Vesuvius, escalating one production incident into a major catastrophe. Finally, Lisa, who occupied the office next to her father, confronted him. "What's going on with you?" she pressed. "I've never seen you like this!"

"This is more than I can handle," he finally confided.

By late spring, he sought help. The counseling helped diminish his sense of all-consuming rage, but the consequences of the incarceration stoked an even greater fire in Larry.

Release from the German prison left the original issue unresolved: Larry had had an unwarranted arrest warrant against him that had remained a matter of record — for three more years. Hertz, clearly at fault, had never taken measures to correct the problem. Even now, the warrant remained in place, so reentering Germany to pursue business was out of the question for Larry. No amount of letter writing or phone calls remedied the trouble. His pleas of distress left no impression. Larry's only option: fight them in court.

Ironically, Hertz had been a Pantone client. In 1967, during the recognition and growth of corporate identity, Hertz decided to adjust and standardize its corporate 'yellow,' and turned to Pantone for reformulation. That relationship, however, seemed long forgotten.

The five-day trial finally began in 1980. Hertz's attorneys argued for a change of venue. The case, they felt, should be tried in Germany, where the incident took place. Larry was incredulous. *How dare they*, he thought! The judge denied their request.

Lisa and Richard attended the trial. Vicky, who already begun attending college in Arizona, received daily reports from her sister. Intellectually, Larry had no problem with his children hearing the details surrounding the Hertz matter and what had happened to him as a result of it. But when it came time for the court appointed psychiatrist to convey his evaluation, he requested that Lisa and Richard not attend.

"I wasn't embarrassed about them finding out that I couldn't sleep and the like," rationalizes Larry. "But I didn't want them to hear about how I broke down in front of him and sobbed like a baby. I don't know, I guess it's because you perceive yourself as a strong person. Maybe it was my pride or ego. But when something as terrifying as this happens to you, it all goes away. I'm their father. You know, daddy is supposed to be strong." His children never questioned his judgment.

Practically an open-and-shut case, irrefutable, the judge awarded Larry a substantial monetary judgment. More importantly, with the warrant lifted, Larry felt the weight of persecution and undue pressure lift. He could breathe a sigh of relief and return to life and work.

During that time, another matter also finally resolved. When Larry's divorce decree became final, the officially single man submerged himself in one activity after another. He night-clubbed during the week at venues like Studio 54 and sunned, surfed and partied on weekends with friends and family at his Bridgehampton home. Wealthy, erudite, debonair, with an impish grin and a twinkle in his eye — a bit like Errol Flynn — he recognized his appeal to women but contended that his revolving door of girlfriends was merely arm candy.

By summer's end 1977, Lisa would be returning to college and Vicky would begin her first year at Boston University. For the first time in ages, a calm appeared on the family front. Work was still hectic. It always required his attention. Even girlfriends, conjectured Larry, had to take a back seat to mistress Pantone. Still, Larry felt back in control.

Then, on August 18 at 12:30 a.m., a phone call turned his new life inside out.

"Daddy, it's Lisa."

Earlier that evening, Vicky had argued with her mother about using the car that she shared with her sister. Vicky wanted to say goodbye to friends before leaving for Boston University, but Lisa had planned to drive to Bridgehampton that night. Larry thought the phone call was a continuation of the squabble.

It wasn't.

"Vicky's been in an auto accident. We're on our way to the hospital. She's been taken to Nyack Hospital by ambulance."

He would later find out that the two sisters had agreed that Vicky would take the BMW with the promise of a timely return. While out with her friend, Julia, Vicky lost track of time, realized she should have already left for home, and in Cinderella fashion, jumped into the car and sped off. Just a few miles from her New City home, the back end of the car fishtailed on a curve. She desperately tried to correct but lost control and hit a telephone poll, sheering off the driver's side of the car and crushing the driver's seat to a quarter of its regular size. Though her friend, Julia, walked away unharmed, Vicky was thrown to the pavement. Now the eighteen-year-old, who looked like a young ballerina, rode bikes, climbed mountains and water-skied like a champion, lay unconscious.

Larry thought his heart had stopped, but the pounding in his ears told him otherwise.

"I'll be up, Lisa. I just want to make a few phone calls first."

Ever the problem-solver, the fixer, Larry leapt into action on Vicky's behalf. Concerned for her immediate care and certain that a New York hospital could offer his daughter a better chance for recovery, he spent the rest of the night calling specialists and lining up a helicopter to transport Vicky to Manhattan. By then, however, Vicky's medical team had done all they could to stabilize her. Only time would tell if Vicky, who had been due to enter college, would be all right.

"For the next forty-eight to seventy-two hours, it's really out of our hands," the doctor had said.

Larry, a man to whom the word wait was obscene, would have to do just that.

By 5 a.m., adrenalin pulsing through him, he showered, dressed and drove to Nyack where the family stood vigil. For three days, as he sat by Vicky's side, he waited for a sign that his daughter was improving. None came. He asked and waited for answers, but none came. His frustration finally peaked as he sat by the riverbank eating his lunch. He threw his hamburger into the trash and picked up his old I'm-not-going-to-take-it-anymore attitude. Returning to the hospital, he insisted that he be given an assessment. Would she get better? Would she remain in a vegetative state? He wanted — no, demanded — a daily progress report.

For three weeks, Vicky remained the same. For three weeks Larry abandoned the office to sit by her side, thoughts of his own trauma in Germany all but erased.

I had problems? he thought. *Not really. Not compared to Vicky, lying so still, wavering between life and death.*

As he walked about the hospital, sometimes reflective and meditative, Larry's mind oftentimes just wandered. He recalled the story he had heard about why operating rooms were green. Based on the Laws of Simultaneous Contrast (Michel Eugene Chevreul, 1839), the cones in your eyes need equilibrium. Whenever you stare at a particular color and then look away, particularly at a white background, the cones in your eyes generate the opposite color. In 1920, Doctor Harry M. Sherman wrote a paper, "The Green Operating Room at St. Luke's Hospital," where he suggested certain changes. The contrast of the red wound tissue and the green flash it produced on the white walls rendered the eye temporarily useless until it had time to readjust. To overcome the effect, Sherman suggested painting the floors and wainscoting green — spinach green to be exact — the direct opposite on the color wheel of blood red. Seeing how this worked to ease the eye, he took the idea one step further by changing the color of the patient wound draping to green and finally, the operating theater scrubs as well.[21]

At the end of a third long week, Vicky finally opened her eyes. She uttered no words, made no movements. But she was back. It took her days to show, with a small nod of her head, that she could hear her family.

Vicky had suffered some brain stem edema — a swelling of the

[21] *http://www.colormatters.com/news_may05/*

spinal cord that can cause the constricted cord to destroy itself. Other injuries included scrapes, bruises and swelling. Long after she had learned to move her body again, her right arm remained semi-paralyzed.

After her release, Vicky returned to her mother's house unable to walk or to speak clearly. Though she embarked on intensive speech and physical therapy, her progress seemed slow, and she remained under round-the-clock nursing supervision.

Unable to attend college and increasingly static under her mother's overly-attentive care, she had retreated from life — but not by choice. The brain stem injury she suffered had diminished the once active and athletic teen but not broken her spirit.

"I want to *live* again," Vicky would vehemently tell her mother. "I don't need nurses anymore."

Caught between the happiness of his child and the lack of a solution, Larry again turned to the child psychologist who had helped during the separation. "Drastic change" were the words that rang in Larry's ears. He concurred after recalling comments that Vicky had made about her isolation and the frequent rows with her mother over her care.

"She mothers me too much," Vicky complained to Larry.

Larry called her to make a date for Sunday brunch at the Rainbow Room. He would use this occasion to speak with her. Besides, he supposed that the outing would make Vicky feel better. Her handicap, however, presented an obstacle. What if she needed to go to the ladies' room? This was a situation only a female could handle, so Larry called a long-time friend, explained the situation and invited her to join them.

Excitedly, Vicky dressed for the occasion. Larry picked her up. During brunch, he broached the delicate topic.

"Vicky, why don't you think about coming to live with me in Manhattan?"

She glanced out the window at the city shining in the mid-morning sun, and a gradual smile lit her face.

"I thought you'd never ask," she said, struggling to get her tongue around the words that still proved a challenge.

"Kid, you have a deal," Larry exclaimed.

"But Dad, won't I interfere with your life?" she countered, well aware of his man-about-town ways.

Larry knew his separation from their mother had taken its toll on his children. They clearly had felt that he took them off the shelf when he had time for them, then put them back up when he was done.

"You mean I really can come?" Vicky asked with a smile that would have moved Larry to tears, if he had allowed it.

"On one condition," he said, his words sounding like a B-movie, even to himself. "This is not going to be a hayride. You're going to come to my place and work your (gorgeous) little ass off. You're going to be up at 8:00 a.m. every morning. You're going to have physical therapy, speech therapy, psychotherapy, educational therapy, every damn therapy we can get for you. You're going to be on a full schedule so that by the time it's bedtime, you're going to faint yourself into bed."

Vicky looked at him; a great deal of thought punctuated her silence. "That's okay," she agreed.

By the end of October, Vicky had moved into Larry's 23rd floor Olympic Tower apartment. He arranged for his housekeeper, Julia, to work full-time escorting Vicky to her various therapies during the day. Each evening he arrived home in time to dine and spend the evening with Vicky. Often exhausted from a full day of therapy, she would retire early, allowing Larry to turn his attention back to Pantone.

Living the life of the well-to-do, handsome bachelor had halted for a time, but as Vicky's schedules stabilized, he returned to dating, guardedly at first, then openly as time passed. For Vicky, this was a double-edged sword. The beautiful women who came through the apartment, some merely ten years older than she, made quite an impression on her. On the mend physically, the unmanicured, petite brunette began to take care of herself, eat better, dress with panache. Still, jealousy welled up, and Vicky occasionally overreacted (slammed doors) when Larry entertained at home.

"She needs a life," Larry thought. She had worked very hard and made a conscious effort to get better. She had made him very proud, but she needed to get back into the mainstream.

Vicky wanted to go to college, and Larry agreed that she was ready. As a member of the Board of Trustees at Hofstra University, he was able to enroll Vicky at their University Without Walls program for a semester while she continued to recuperate. This awakened her to possibilities and, in the fall of 1978, she began a limited college program at New York University. Remarkably, the young woman, once unable to speak or even dress herself, traveled alone to classes, sending her mother into a temporary frenzy. Eventually, her determined journey forward would carry her to Arizona State University, where she would receive her Bachelors degree in 1982.

Even during the toughest part of Vicky's recovery, Larry's renewed fathering obligations hadn't distracted him from his baby, Pantone. He had protected what he had already achieved and set his goals on expansion and diversification through licensing. He had contracted with Letraset, the makers of tack-down letters for graphic designers, for worldwide rights to manufacture and sell graphic arts materials.

Larry's philosophy — when life hands you lemons, you make PANTONE 100 — continued to serve him well. He signed a licensing arrangement with the DayGlo Color Corporation: he added fluorescent-based formulas to the books, which DayGlo created and sold, and for which they paid royalties to Pantone.

Sales of the color books and licensing royalties had kept the company flush. Larry, of course, wanted more for the upcoming decade. During all the years he had worked as a color matcher for print, advertising and packaging, one thing had become clear — color significantly impacted peoples' lives. There had to be a way to link the name Pantone — the company that had brought consistent, reproducible color to individuals and industries — with product directed to the consumer.

11

Cashing in on Color

For Pantone to cash in on the impact of color, a potentially exciting new revenue-maker, there had to be believers and buyers. The time had come to create a new level of interest.

Through his work with the American Film Institute in Los Angeles, Larry met Henry Rogers, partner in the leading public relations firm, Rogers and Cowan. Somehow, Henry Rogers and Dick Taylor — the dynamic duo of PR who had just delved into corporate work — saw in Pantone a commodity that should become a more consumer-friendly rather than strictly industrial brand. The two envisioned a very aggressive public relations strategy to educate the consumer about color, the importance of color, and why color matters. Larry eyed Pantone's future while Henry arranged it.

"Larry, I'd like you to come out to L.A. I've set up a meeting with Paige Rense of *Architectural Digest*. We should talk to her about creating an association with Pantone."

The three sat down to lunch at the Hillcrest Country Club

restaurant. Over Cobb salads, they discussed a possible alliance. Paige recognized Pantone's importance. Color was, after all, an integral part of the magazine's work. Nevertheless, for her, the name of Pantone didn't carry the cachet of the magazine. Pantone needed influence and credibility outside its sphere. At that moment, Henry Rogers threw out an idea.

"We are planning an arm of Pantone that would generate research and information and be a repository of color knowledge."

Though *Architectural Digest* would not commit to the alliance, Henry and Larry moved quickly to initiate the plan. Within months, they formed an advisory board and introduced what would become Pantone's strongest PR weapon — the Pantone Color Institute® launched to compile research on the psychology of color, societal trends and the manner in which individuals react to color. Pantone needed someone with an inside track on color-reliant industries and a working knowledge of color psychology.

Upon graduation in 1982, Vicky had returned to the Pantone fold, initially working as a floater. Though she considered herself an artist at heart, "if they needed telemarketing for the graphics division, I would work there. If they needed it for the new professional color division (the future textile division), well…"

She hated floating, hated telemarketing even more. Vicky much preferred joining Lisa and Richard in the loft where they worked on the textile system, cutting up swatches and chips and placing them in color spaces on the easels. "I could relate to that," remarks Vicky.

"I'm a visual person. When the Institute came along, I was excited to be part of the startup."

While Rogers and Larry began their search for a talking head, Vicky collected color information, anecdotes and history. Vicky spent countless hours in the vast New York City libraries. In the days before digitized library information, when patrons culled card catalogs, wrote down numbers, and handed slips to librarians who then pulled books from the stacks, she awaited her selections to peruse. "Bookmarked pages were copied for you," comments Vicky on the long days that turned to weeks. "The process was tedious. Interesting but tedious."

Initially part of the PR department, the gathered and categorized data proved important for Lisa's upcoming newsletter, *Color News*, which freely dispensed information to the unenlightened about the psychology and use of color. Admittedly a venue to help position Pantone as the color authority, Lisa also used it to reach and influence everyone who used color.

Vicky supplied color teasers like:

- Poultry farmers infuse chicken feed with marigold petals to give the chickens a healthy golden glow.
- Black pasta served in chic restaurants is made by mixing squid or cuttlefish ink to the dough. It's also used in sepia toner for photos.
- Rumor has it that when NFL's Philadelphia Eagles lined up for new uniforms, the owner of the team insisted that the color matched the green of his wife's Jaguar.

With billions of dollars riding on color decisions in product development, more and more companies began calling Pantone for its advice. Mike Salvato of W.L. Gore & Associates, Inc., maker of GORE-TEX® and Windstopper fabrics, for example, contacted Pantone to find technical documentation concerning the best color for a person to wear to maximize their chances of being found during search-and-rescue operations at sea. Vicky, of the Pantone Consulting Services, pointed Salvato to Dr. Thomas Amerson, a vision and human factors researcher at the Naval Submarine Medical Research Lab (NSMRL) working at the U.S. Coast Guard Research and Development Center in Groton, Connecticut. The reports Dr. Amerson provided specified that neon orange was a person's best bet in such a situation.

The Pantone Consulting Services provided additional assistance by matching PANTONE Colors to those described in the reports. Once W.L. Gore's customer approved one of the chips as a best match to current search-and-rescue equipment, the PANTONE Chip provided guidance to the textile dye house to help create the product for their customer. The fluorescent color, called "hunter" orange or international orange because it increases visibility, is also said to have decreased hunting accidents from mistaken gun shots.[22]

Late in 1982, Pantone officially launched the Pantone Color Institute with a lavish breakfast for media and design moguls at New

[22] *Hunting-Associated Injuries and Wearing "HUNTER" ORANGE CLOTHING — New York 1989-1995; Morbidity and Mortality Weekly Report, Oct 18, 1996.*

York's newest restaurant, Maxim's. "Rogers and Cowen was about glitz and glamour, and we really followed their lead," recalls Lisa. The Institute (later morphed into the Consulting Division) which offered information and research on how color influences human thought, emotions and physical reactions and how businesses could use color more effectively, cemented Pantone's reputation as a color authority. Pantone's new research division brought others looking for expertise specifically tailored to their brands. When ING Financial initially considered their national color, orange, for their logo, many voiced concerns that they would not be taken seriously. It had been a color associated with things of lesser value, not an idea to convey in a financial institution. A color used for its visibility factor, orange is often associated with high energy and, like red, can be a stimulant. Uncertain, ING turned to Pantone for clarification and verification. Would orange have negative repercussions? Had any other financial institutions used the color?

Vicky investigated. The resulting data showed that orange had indeed been used successfully by other financial institutions. The color had surged and attracted up-market clients as well as a younger audience. Reassured that the fresh, youthful appearance of orange would garner the attention ING desired and pleased because it also represented the color of Holland's national flower — the tulip — the company activated its plan. Today, their orange logo catches the eye as a prominent part of every publicity campaign.

Resolutely important, color may be the single fastest growing and valuable factor in logo design and brand identity. Orange, a particularly hot color used for branding and packaging in the mid-2000s, incited companies to battle for 'orange' territory just as they had battled for 'blue' real estate. In 1994, the U.K. telecommunications company, **orange**, was launched. The trademarked name that researchers called fun, lively, distinctive and fresh was encased in an orange square. Along came EasyMobile with their bright orange logo used by other EasyGroup companies. Orange, the company, immediately took up the cause in 2005, accusing EasyMobile of engaging in a form of trademark infringement known as 'passing off' in which a new company tries to ride an established player's coattails and confuse the consumer into thinking the two businesses are connected. This legal battle was the first in the U.K. waged over a corporate color.

The fight for orange represents how profitable the right color can be. Conversely, "Being wrong with color can really hurt you," Anne Cashill, vice president of merchandising at Liz Claiborne, which manufactures Kenneth Cole Sportswear, DKNY Jeans, and sixteen other national brands, told *Wired* magazine. "We subscribe to the same color services as the Gap, club Monaco, and Ralph Lauren. It's a good thing to be different, but it's not a good thing to be completely in left field."

The case with Munsingwear exemplifies this claim. For their holiday 1982 men's collection, the active wear manufacturer decided to veer from its time-tested color selections and offer sea green and grape. The new colors did not sell, teaching the company a valuable lessen about color consistency.

"Designers have such a tough job, particularly the ones working for big corporations," says Lisa. "It's so risky — millions of dollars depend on their decisions. Everyone wants to know the *why* behind what's going on with color — and they all have to justify their color choices to management." Pantone could help them do that.

Ad agencies and marketing firms turned with increasing frequency to Pantone for color validation. One major credit card company had hired a corporate identity firm to modify its traditional logo colors. "They came to us to get a third-party opinion of the colors. Based on how they were going to be used, they wanted to know 'Would these colors be appropriate for the industry then and five years out?'" Richard recalls. "We ended up changing one of the colors. It wasn't as serious as it could have been because we caught it before they went public."

One product introduced in the late 1990s, a board game called "Perfect Wedding" geared to girls age five to seven seemed to have everything going for it. The packaging portrayed a brunette bride, the engagement ring and the wedding cake-top bridal couple. However, the slightest mistake in the groom's hair, making it appear gray, left sales flat.

Ironically, the Pantone Color Institute would remain without a leader for three years. The long search for a voice concluded after Larry read *Alive with Color* (1985) by Leatrice Eiseman (Lee). He recognized the value of her expertise. She could bring Pantone credibility with credentials in psychology, fashion and interior design. The alliance proved beneficial for both parties. Lee introduced the psychology of color to the consumer, garnering attention for Pantone as a brand, and for herself as a color guru.

As Lee's right-hand person, Vicky's research intensified — gathering information and tracking trends that supported Lee's color seminars. The psychology of color, whether real or contrived, held strong convictions. Color, the great non-verbal communicator, relied upon by designers and manufacturers alike, was a selling tool and, the family's business was to create and sell tools.

To reach this position of accepted color authority, the Institute's promotional activities in the mid to late 1980s accelerated, along with an outpouring of money, always a sore spot for Larry. Lisa, who worked the public relations angle, explains, "It was always a fight to get him to spend the money on promotional events and brand building. I must be his alter ego, though — I *could* spend it. So he could let the onus fall on me."

Resistance aside, Larry could not deny the fact that companies had begun to recognize the importance of brand identity and to spend a lot of money creating an image. To become a part of the new wave, he would have to do that too. Pantone, however, was a uniquely unclassifiable business whose partners — the printers and ink manufacturers — had no interest in branding their names. The Pantone Color Institute helped Larry focus attention on company growth.

As part of its promotional plan in 1985, the Pantone Color Institute launched its first color awards honoring up-and-coming talent for innovative use of color in graphics, interiors, fashion and industrial design. The advisory board was comprised of over 60 such luminaries in the areas of the interior and industrial design, architecture, textile, fashion, cosmetics, advertising and graphic design. Names that graced the list included Donna Karan, Oscar de la Renta, Adrien Arpel, Santo Loquasto, Milton Glaser, Vicente Wolf and Gene Federico, who guided the Institute's choices and presented the awards at the newly renovated Rainbow Room.

Larry reveled in the media coverage, a trait he seems to have passed on to daughter Lisa. He granted interviews while Leatrice Eiseman booked speaking engagements and Vicky busily fielded color queries:

- *What is the derivation of Khaki?* Answer: British soldiers serving in India proved too visible (not to mention uncomfortable) in their reddish uniforms. Khaki-colored uniforms were first adopted for British troops serving under Brigadier Sir Henry Burnett Lumsden in 1848. The word 'khaki' comes from the Persian (Urdu) 'khak' and means dust or earth-colored. (History)
- *What is America's favorite color?* Answer: Hands down, Americans prefer blue. Red comes in a distant second.
- *Why is it harder to distinguish colors as a person gets older?* Answer: As a person ages the eye's lens yellows so colors cannot be perceived the same way as in youth. Bright colors don't seem

as bright, making pastels more appealing. (Science)

- ***Why do baby boys wear blue and baby girls wear pink?***
Answer: An early study by Joseph Jastrow, professor of psychology at the University of Wisconsin (1897), holds true in our minds even today: men prefer blue and women prefer red (pink). History contradicts this blue/pink gender issue. In the 18th century, pink was introduced for children's clothing...but for infant boys rather than girls, as it was considered a cousin of the bold, powerful red! In 1914, an American newspaper advised mothers, "...use pink for the boy and blue for the girl, if you are a follower of convention."[23] The Ladies' Home Journal, bible to the American homemaker, decreed in its June 1918 edition that to differentiate newborns, "There has been a great diversity of opinion on the subject, but the generally accepted rule is pink for the boy and blue for the girl. The reason is that pink being a more decided and stronger color is more suitable for the boy, while blue, which is more delicate and dainty, is prettier for the girl." (History, psychology)

The Institute's accomplishments reinforced Larry's sense that the company was moving in the right direction. His mantra, "We need a sense of urgency," which floats around the offices today, helped place Pantone on top of the color hierarchy, with Larry as its

---

[23] *The Sunday Sentinel, March 29, 1914.*

IN A PICKLE

Food colorants are safe today but the practice of coloring food to disguise its poor quality or enhance its looks dates back 3,000 years. Unfortunately some of the processes had deadly consequences. In Frederick Accum's 1820 "A Treatise on Adulterations of Food and Culinary Poisons," he noted the following practices in London:

Pickles owed their green color to copper sulfate, a deadly poison.

Candy colors came from highly toxic salts of copper and lead.

Thorn leaves, dried and covered with verdigris (copper oxide) were sold as Chinese tea.

Spent tea leaves were tinted with black lead and other chemicals, dried and sold as fresh tea.

Gloucester cheese owed its orange color from the addition of poisonous red lead.

leader. From Bell Communications to BIC® pens, Claussen pickles to the U.S. Army, Pantone helped companies make the most apt color choice for product development, packaging, logos and identification, as well as interior and exterior design.

Pantone also helped companies solve color-related reproduction problems. "Color is a deeply illusive property, capable of shifting under the most minute change in conditions," writes *I.D.* magazine's Tom Vanderbilt. "In essence, color acts like a living organism responding to fluctuations in its surroundings."[24]

Problems arose in the medium of print all the time. Larry had discovered this earlier while working with ink on paper.

Color emblazoned directly on metal proved especially problematic, as both Anheuser Busch and Eastern Airlines discovered.

The world-famous brewer suffered millions of dollars in returns because color faded cans of Budweiser beer prompted customers to assume the product was old and stale. Pantone's Packaging Standards Program, still used today, solved the problem.

As early as 1964, Larry worked with Eastern Airlines when its Caribbean bound planes, newly clad in a dark blue, began to turn purple. Larry discovered that the paint pigment Eastern Airlines had selected destabilized at 75 degrees below zero and 110 degrees in the desert. Invited by Max Heisig, their corporate identity consultant, Larry flew to Miami to confer with the aircraft paint manufacturer to help solve the problem. The result: the original paint was too highly saturated with pigment and not balanced with sufficient protective varnish. Their new aircraft color, Ionosphere Blue, also became the new corporate color formulated by Larry for all other applications.

Working with companies became an integral part of Pantone's business. Problem solving, not the most lucrative portion of Pantone's bottom line, kept Larry diversified. The general queries directed to the Institute required an inordinate amount of research

---

[24] *Vanderbilt, Tom, I.D. Magazine, May 2000.*

into the history, sociology, science and psychology of color, led mainly by Vicky, and all were answered free of charge. Yet Vicky felt that the Institute, despite being a not-for-profit division, needed to cover its costs, so she approached Larry with a proposal to sell the information and to aid companies in their color choices.

THE KING *of* COLOR

12

The Business of Color

Companies rely on our nearly innate, emotional responses to color when they present their products and services to us.

Some color selections may be obvious. The Mattel Corporation chose pink for their trademark Barbie for Girls line — not a soft baby pink or bubble gum pink, but PANTONE 820, a hot, vibrant, attention-getting pink. Fashionista Elsa Schiaparelli coined the term "shocking pink," which describes the color perfectly.

Not so obvious may be the blue package of Oreo cookies (originally gold in 1912) given that blue does not occur naturally in food that's safe to eat. Even blueberries aren't blue but a deep purple. The belief that blue food is poisonous possibly dates to the blue bottles relegated to holding poisons. Yet, who wouldn't recognize a bag of Oreos?

Some have disagreed with the notion that colors affect us psychologically or physiologically. David Canter, professor of applied psychology at Surrey University, once said that color has no direct influence on us, that it simply "makes things more attractive and interesting, and carries information in a complex world."[25]

Make them attractive and interesting enough, however, and our behavior is altered. Directly impacted by color, purchase decisions are determined in the first .03 seconds upon visual impact, another reason why red dominates our consumer shelves. Yellow, the brightest color to impact the human eye, also weighs in on our buying choices.

Yellow sends more neural signals than either end of the spectrum (red and violet), tending to catch our eye more quickly. So when direct mail solicitations appear in black type on a yellow background, responses increase significantly.

The message may be subliminal, but the effect is clear. In the case of yellow, the most recognizable color in most cultures, we are reminded of sunshine, lightness, warmth and happiness and are more likely to purchase an item we feel would make our lives better, easier, more pleasant. The effects of color appear to show no age barriers. When children are told a happy story and asked to draw about it afterward, they defer to a yellow crayon.

Ironically, as a visible cue, color can backfire, as in the following case with yellow. In 1984, when asked about the Nature Made vitamin containers, people overwhelmingly mistook the yellow container with black and white labeling for ant poison. Still, citing Pantone research, a 1999 "Costco Connection" article[26] predicted that yellow

---

[25] *Tysoe, Maryon; What's Wrong With Blue Potatoes; Psychology Today, December 1985, vol 19, page 6(2).*
[26] *"Costco Connection," December 1999.*

"may be taking over the marketing world…Tests show that [a yellow background with black type] scores the highest in memory retention and in legibility."

As a means of remembering their products, manufacturers and marketers choose color. We retain color information more readily than verbal or aural cues. As such, researchers at the American Society for Training & Development concluded that color can enhance memory retention when it comes to organizing ideas or recalling details. Dr. Charles Allen of the University of Montana Psychology Department explained, though words may be associated with them, "colors are represented in memory in a different way…" This is clear when we cannot remember on which floor we parked our car but can remember a color designation. Further, when a word is isolated by a color, especially red, its retention is significantly higher. This suggests that product branding and labeling with the right color improves salability. Think about Healthy Choice products. What do you remember? The green packaging.

Because of the impact of color on consumers and sales, fortunes are spent to achieve just the right presentation when initiating products based on the notion of the meaning of colors. Dove soap couldn't be anything but white, pure and clean. Around 1989, the makers of Ty-D-Bol toilet bowl cleanser changed the bottle from light blue and green to white with bold lettering, thereby increasing sales some 40 percent. They revitalized the packaging once again some years later,

GOLDEN BROWNS

We can thank the color brown for the first color standard measuring device. In Color: A Natural History of the Palette, *author Finlay tells the story of Joseph Lovibond, a young Englishman gold-mining in Australia who unwittingly lost his fortune in the Sydney Harbor. He returned home and joined his family's beer brewing business. As he began to categorize the brews, he realized that color was the key to separating them and that he needed a grading scale. Several experiments with pigment proved disappointing, so he turned to stained glass shades of brown as a standard against which to compare his brews. From this, the first colorimeter was devised in 1885 as a scale for his browns, and then later adapted it to measure the primary colors — red, yellow and blue. If you want to know how your beer rates, you can look it up on the Lovibond Beer Color Database.[27]*

retaining the white bottle and replacing the dark background logo with a "confident Ty-D-Bol Man riding a new wave [blue] of cleaning Performance."[28]

Some companies use color to stand out in a crowded field. The original packaging for the Green Giant products portrayed the Jolly Green Giant on a white label. Once frozen vegetables were intro-

[27] *http://www.cis.rit.edu/fairchild/lovibond.htm*
[28] *Hanson Associates, Inc.; http://www.hansondesign.com/pages/tydbol_news.html*

duced by Green Giant and its competitors, such as Birds Eye and Stouffer's, the white background became synonymous with 'generic,' so the Green Giant Company changed its packaging colors to a "sea of green" to reflect freshness and offer a consistent look within its product line. Green, previously associated with mold and fungus — food gone bad — had never been used with food products until Healthy Choice packaging. Green has since come to signify fresh, organic and healthy.

Until the comeback of coffee, chocolate and eco-thinking, brown was a less likely color choice for a company product. Yet, UPS has used the proprietary PANTONE Color for years. Some claim the original color was chosen to mimic the upscale look of the era's Pullman train cars, others that it was to intended to obscure dirt on their trucks. Either way, it's become a major part of their marketing campaign. "What can brown do for you?"

And can you imagine Hershey's Milk Chocolate wrapped in anything but brown? The Hershey Company never did. Indeed, to ensure a consistent look for their trademark brown wrapper when printed on paper, for years the brown ink color was applied over a coat of silver color to prevent absorption.

Our responses to specific shades are so visceral that industries spend millions testing for results. They simply cannot afford mistakes in a competitive environment, especially since those mistakes can cost companies massive fortunes in printing and product presentation, to say nothing of product sales. But that doesn't always guarantee success.

Years ago, a Swiss designer repackaged an instant coffee brand for a manufacturer. His design won a prize. Yet the color he selected for the entire presentation, labels, packaging and displays — mauve — caused sales to plummet and the manufacturer to go back to the drawing board.[29] It simply was the wrong color for coffee. "It's understandable. I would never have chosen mauve," quips Lee Eiseman. The designer would have known, too, if he had consulted Pantone.

On the other hand, who could have predicted that Heinz would sell $23 million in green ketchup?

Understanding color responses and preferences, economic trends and cultural cycles provides data for the design community and fodder for the marketers. Had Larry stood idly by, relying solely on his fan books and ancillary art and graphic design products, he might have missed the greater arena. The licensing contract that came about with 3M, which had taken several years to secure, provided Larry with the final impetus to expand Pantone's services to yet another level: corporate brand identity and consulting.

Companies use colors to connect with consumers. When it comes to corporate identity, the stakes, as we have seen, are high. So are the rewards when the choice is right, for branding color brands the corporate identity or the product into our consciousness. How and why color choices are made becomes more obvious when we

---

[29] *Publication Information: Article Title: What's Wrong with Blue Potatoes. Contributors Maryon Tysoe — author Magazine Title: Psychology Today Volume 19. Publication Date: December 1985. Page Number 6+. COPYRIGHT 1985 Sussex Publishers, Inc.; COPYRIGHT 2002 Gale Group.*

look at choices that have clearly succeeded, and the history behind the color they chose.

Caterpillar tractors and Stanley Tools are unmistakably bright sunshine yellow. Perceived as the most intense color in the spectrum — and a definite attention grabber as mentioned in the Costco Connection article predicting that yellow would take over the marketing world. The color's brightness factor makes New York City taxis more noticeable in traffic, a message learned from nineteenth-century horse-drawn coaches in Paris. Yellow also signifies caution. When the signal light turns yellow, it alerts us about an impending stop. A yellow school bus is more highly visible, making us more cognizant of nearby children. Yellow also warns us of danger or quarantine. Ironically, Larry discovered that Kodak's trademarked yellow-and-black box contained toxic chromium yellow pigment. Though highly unlikely to cause death or even illness after ingesting one box, Larry nevertheless reformulated the signature shade of yellow.

John Deere, appropriately, prefers the green of nature and fertility but most likely had no choice because green was the first color to be stabilized for outdoor use. As with Caterpillar, the company choice of color is regularly validated by clients who, instead of referring to the machinery by name when ordering from distributors, simply say, "I'll take two yellows and one green."

When BP Oil set out to create a company logo, they wanted people to perceive BP as non-nature-threatening. What better nature color is there than green? They also wanted to project themselves as forward thinking and energetic. Thus, yellow and green move out in a sunflower pattern.

Green, in all its iterations, also reminds us of leisure (which, incidentally, includes money), prompting companies like Starbucks (relax and have a coffee), Barnes & Noble (relax and read a book), J. Crew (relax in our clothes) and H&R Block (relax, we'll save you money) to opt for the color. Napoleon's favorite color, emerald green, hailed from Germany around 1800. The rich hue covered all the walls of his home-in-exile in St. Helena. Produced by combining verdigris and copper arsenate, it made one of the deadliest poisons ever devised. Though relaxing, its undetectable fumes eventually took Napoleon's life. Japanese Emperor Hirohito's experience with the color was much more in keeping with its innate calming message. He loved his soothing garden so much that to honor his birthday each year, celebrants refer to it as 'Green Day.'

Purple, a favorite of Cleopatra's and historically aligned with royalty, speaks for the up-market English shop Asprey. Seen as representing contemplation and imagination, Leonardo da Vinci believed that the power of meditation increased ten times under purple light, like that from stained glass. The color — regaled in the 1960s and early 1970s by such rock-and-roll icons as Jimi Hendrix with his "Purple Haze" album, and the band Deep Purple, and commemorated a few years prior in the top of the charts hit "Purple People Eater" — had already been adopted by M&M candies, removed in 1949 in favor of tan, and subsequently reinstated by a vote of fans across the globe.

The early 2000s revived purple for branding purposes. It was different and hip, even making its way into political campaigns when Ken Livingstone of the Labour Party used purple for his victorious London mayoral campaign.

Author Alice Walker, in *The Color Purple*, conveys the color's imperial status in the scene when Celia picks out a dress for her best friend Shug. "I think what color Shug Averry would wear. She like a queen to me so I say…Somethin' purple…" Clearly Walker has a penchant for this particular color. "I think it pisses God off if you walk by the color purple in a field somewhere and don't notice," she claims through her character.

Red, which includes shades from Oscar Mayer burgundy (actually metallicized red) to tomato red, is a highly visible, appetite-stimulating color. That explains why it represents a major percentage of supermarket shelf products. Where 7-Up is concerned, it proved a way for the clear, clean, refreshing soda had to make a visible splash in a field crowded with colas. The red dot on the white and green background adds an unexpected surprise — vibrancy, especially against its complement — green.

One of only three true colors that cannot be created by mixing ink or paint with any other color, pure red is used to convey excitement and energy.[30] Puma International, the athletic wear company, uses a red in its logo — PANTONE 485 (also the color of the Mastercard red circle) — printed twice for vibrancy to signify

---

[30] *The other two true colors when talking about mixing pigment are yellow and blue.*

strength, dynamism and athleticism. Perhaps they knew that a red flag during Roman times signified battle. Possibly for the same reason, Smirnoff Vodka, awarded the title of Official Purveyor to the Imperial Russian Court in 1886, enlists the red Russian coat of arms on its label. On the other hand, the Russian word for red originally meant beautiful.

Still, a predominant percentage of American companies, especially those currently or once skewed towards men, opt for blue. We can't think about IBM, for example, without associating the color blue (though in reality the formula for this PANTONE Shade of blue mixes in violet as well).

America's favorite color hasn't always enjoyed such an exalted place in colordom. During the Middle Ages, although Indian indigo was brought to Europe by Vasco de Gama, a more available and affordable version of the color was manufactured from woad, an herb in the mustard family. The use of woad seeds dates to the Neolithic period and have been found in the French cave of l'Audoste, Bouches du Rhone (France). Undoubtedly used for its astringent quality, it healed wounds quickly, perhaps another reason why the Picts painted their bodies with it.

Indeed, a ban on using indigo to dye textiles blue was levied in order to protect local peasants from foreign competition. Using woad, the dye derived from the plant of the same name, however, was nasty business. The process required dyers to consume massive amounts of alcohol and mix their urine with the dye, rendering the dyers pretty much useless come Monday morning. Thus the expression "blue Monday."

Despite the lowly history of blue, major corporations spend millions fashioning logos, vying for that small bit of real estate within the blue spectrum, while still trying to differentiate from one another, according to *Wired* magazine.[31] Why the fuss? Blue apparently imparts a sense of reliability, steadfastness and truth. Perhaps that's why police officers are referred to as 'men in blue.'

Traditionally a favorite color of the male gender (and royals), not only is blue the preferred color for male dominated businesses, it rules among NFL football uniforms with half of the thirty-two teams sporting blue. This gender domination may explain why blue and business have become synonymous. When CBS news decided to test consumers' familiarity with various blues used by retailers, they discovered that mall shoppers overwhelmingly recognized GAP blue (PANTONE 492) above all others. The color was so recognizable, in fact, that Gap named its premiere fragrance "492."

Sophisticated shoppers will recognize the soft and distinctive Tiffany hue, a shade chosen by Louis Tiffany back in 1837. When Rita Braver, on the May 1, 2005, CBS Sunday Morning segment, asked John Loring of Tiffany & Company what he thought the color has achieved as a marketing tool, he answered, 'You couldn't possibly measure it worldwide…The blue box with the white ribbon — that

---

[31] *Hertz, J.C..; Living Color, Wired Magazine, June 2003, issue 11.06, p. 167.*

is our number one icon of marketing." As a brand, the color instantly sends the heart racing with anticipation. A challenge to reproduce, the robin's egg blue can easily turn green in production without Pantone adjusting the color used in ads, catalogs, shopping bags and boxes.

These days the notion that color speaks to the masses is a given, and business relies on color to do its talking. Companies know all too well that the choice of corporate colors can make the difference between being in the red or in the black.

Considering the importance of brand identity, why would a Company ever change its color? "We wanted a new color and a refreshed look that demonstrated the changes that H&R Block was making as a company," says Karl Ploeger of H&R Block. Before they chose PANTONE 376 (Granny Smith apple green), they assessed the color using focus groups. Answers to the question "What does this color mean to you?" included comments about spring -which represents growth -and money. Though PANTONE 376 didn't exactly represent a new color group for H&R, since their prior color had also been green, this particular shade did convey a youthful, fresher, more responsive message.

The Weinerschnitzel hot dog chain revamped their color scheme in 1983 from magenta red to orange red to help boost sales of their inexpensive hot dogs. The change was based on the theory that red signals danger, which could repel customers, while orange is associated with "cheap," or, in this case, a less expensive product.

The color that product manufacturers and marketers choose depends a lot on which sex they are selling to, since, as we've seen, colors elicit varied emotional responses between the genders. Though men respond to blue, bright colors attract women more often than darker tones. That reinforces the decision to use bright colors in the packaging of supermarket goods.

Tide laundry detergent, created in the 1950s, stands out among similar products on the supermarket shelves with its distinctively ultra neon orange package. Clearly they communicated something right. The white detergent conveyed cleanliness, and the bold orange brought a sense of power and strength. In terms of marketing, a double hit for cleaner clothes. When asked to rate colors that best convey power in a 1997 survey, the overwhelming majority of respondents chose scarlet red.[32]

With color playing as important a role as it does in customer perception, packaging colors had better be spot-on. A breakdown in corporate communication, however, can jeopardize that in unexpected ways.

General Printing, a customer of Larry's, supplied the red-orange DayGlo ink for the Tide package. Suddenly, the color began to fade and mottle. The makers of Tide blamed the ink formulation for the disaster and contacted Sun Chemical, who, in turn, contacted Larry. By this time, hundreds of thousands of boxes of Tide were bleeding

---

[32] *Heath, Rebecca Piirto and Claudia Montague. "The Wonderful World of Color" Marketing Tools, Oct 1997 v4 n9 p44(7).*

all over grocery shelves.

Not a particularly unusual problem in packaging, Larry had occasionally lent his hand when it came to problems of fading and bleeding colors. As always, he initially focused on the ink recipe.

"What did you change in the ink?"

"Nothing," the technical representative replied. "The formula is exactly the same." He showed it to Larry.

"Did they change the box paper," inquired Larry.

"I asked. They say no," replied the technician.

There was only one option left. The soap's formula had to have been changed. Larry requested an analysis from Tide. Sure enough, the newly formulated soap was bleeding through the paper, thereby affecting the ink. Asking Tide's manufacturers to change their formulation was out of the question. The solution: print an overlay protective coating on the paper product before running the colors through the press. That created a barrier between the product and the ink, preserving Tide's all-important shelf identity.

That capacity to not only help a corporation convey a sales message through color, print the color correctly no matter what the medium, and trouble-shoot any problems that came along would give Pantone an even stronger lock on the color market.

13

The Color Monopoly

Pantone's emergence as a color authority had resulted from years of effort — and not just Larry's. As much as the company had been a one-man show, once Lisa, Richard and Vicky fell into step, their contributions had provided the company with the breadth and depth to turn it from color authority to color monopoly.

Pantone's foray into fashion in the 1980s had given the company the kind of top-secret intelligence consumer product companies drool over. In the process of fulfilling orders, Pantone tracked which colors and swatches were being ordered over and over in response to market demand. The upshot was reams of invaluable data on the hottest colors of the moment. And, at the start of the '80s, colors were indeed hot.

A cacophony of vibrantly saturated, circus-like hues hit the runways in designs sporting banana yellow, ripest raspberry and sun baked orange high waists and short skirts, billowy pants, trompe l'oeil lace prints and big florals, all suggesting the big tent and costume wear. Carnival teal aside, the favorite color for cars for the decade remained gray and appropriately fit the roads when decade end made an abrupt about-face and returned Americans to a palette of sophisticated neutrals and earth tones.

Lisa, whose passion lay in fashion — Manolo Blahniks and designer labels — would play an instrumental role in Pantone's development as the keeper of the color trend information. After graduating from the Fashion Institute of Technology (FIT) with a degree in buying and merchandising, the slender, chic blond headed to New York's garment district as a stylist for hosiery manufacturer Bonny Doon. Though Larry gave his blessing to her pursuits, and even took some responsibility for directing Lisa's vision, he could not dismiss her obvious talent from which Pantone could benefit.

While at the hosiery company, Lisa fearlessly presented new merchandise ideas in her unique way. Rifling through Pantone's Moonachie, New Jersey, warehouse where Letraset shared space, she gathered colored paper for her presentations. She drew on some, cut and arranged others into patterns, and created a collage on a presentation board to accompany her proposed new styles for the upcoming collection and displayed this to the sales and marketing executives of the company. Using this method over and over, she began to notice that graphic design colors didn't always translate into the fashion colors she had in mind for her new product ideas, such as Burberry-style plaid socks in fun colors or pastels. Fashion designers remarked, too, that although they used the PANTONE MATCHING SYSTEM to match fashion colors, even toting it for their European fashion trips to help codify colors they saw, certain seasonal colors were often missing: an array of pastels, pinks and blues and other subtly muted shades of those seen at this time, along with a variety of neutrals. This insight helped prompt what would become one of Pantone's most successful ventures.

During summer breaks from college, Lisa — with brother Richard — had already begun working on the PANTONE Professional Color System®, an expansion of the PANTONE MATCHING SYSTEM originally created for graphic designers. Decorator colors had quickly outpaced colors used to design logos, prompting Larry to acknowledge the need for a new system (the first expansion of the color system in 25 years) for industries involved with fashion, home interiors, architecture — i.e., anything lifestyle-driven.

Personal and household product manufacturers counted on color-conscious Americans to purchase everything from decorator-colored toothbrushes to teapots in colors ranging from Chantal's cobalt blue cookware to pink typewriters from Sharp Electronics.

With his graphics color system already in place, this new project, originally conceived as a consumer color guide for home decorating, was part of Larry's master plan for company expansion. However, he did not consider the project a priority. With no dictated deadline, Lisa and Richard spent their time leisurely collecting color swatches when other work responsibilities didn't interfere. Together, the brother and sister team would drive around gathering bits of color from just about every imaginable source: nature, fabrics, carpeting, paint chips, wall coverings, even cosmetics. Everything, that is, but printed matter.

After amassing some 13,000 color samples and measuring each one on the spectrophotometer to convert it to its color coordinates, they took over the loft space at the Moonachie facility to commence phase two. Though highly technical and counter-intuitive to the creative process, this next stage would test Richard's mettle and capabilities and prove his organization skills.

The duo set up ten oversized easels with gridiron boards representing the Commission Internationale de l'Eclairage three-dimensional color space system. Lisa and Richard painstakingly taped and thumbtacked each of the 13,000 swatches to its corresponding color space coordinate. Certain colors began to amass in areas more than others, a sure sign of popularity. Increasingly high piles, such as beige, indicated a color's usefulness and importance, making it a candidate for the final palette.

Finally, Pantone's color scientist, Al DiBernardo, acquired the 13,000 graph-laden samples. He began to eliminate color redundancies and reduce the quantity to a manageable 1,800. At his side was Mike Garin, who had assisted Larry with the original PANTONE MATCHING SYSTEM in 1963.

As summer wound down, Richard returned to college and Lisa to her other assigned tasks. Lisa, the first Herbert sibling to join Pantone full-time, had, like all three, worked from the ground up learning all aspects of the business. From a bindery position at $100 a week, she moved next to the ink laboratories. Working in quality control for the PANTONE MATCHING SYSTEM Colors, she mixed ink samples to test their formulations. With a spatula, she smeared the ink on a piece of paper to judge the color's strength and transparency. The sample next passed through the spectrophotometer where she matched it against the color 'standard' before going to press. "The toughest part of this job was the first two weeks when I had to get used to the smell of the printing inks, but what I learned was invaluable. It brought me to a greater understanding of what my father had created, how precise and intricate the system was."

Each summer provided new learning experiences for Lisa. Working part-time with the marketing director enabled her to attend trade shows where she handed out posters and information on PANTONE Products. It gave her a sense of Pantone's vigor outside the offices and a chance to interface with clients for the first time.

Still, Lisa's goals rested squarely on the fashion industry rather than on Pantone. Her stint with the hosiery manufacturer that hired her, however, ended abruptly: Lisa wanted to accompany her father to Paris where Vicky had spent the summer before matriculating at New York University. Larry's concern for Vicky's fragile health had prompted his decision to go see his daughter. Lisa, who shared her father's unease, decided to accompany him.

She discussed the possibility with her boss. The trip, she explained, would only be a week and she could shop the local stores typically frequented by designers, collect ideas and bring back samples — all on her own time. When she didn't get the answer she wanted, she concluded that her only recourse was to leave the company. "I felt my boss was being rigid. He knew the situation with my sister, so I told him that family was more important," remarks Lisa.

In need of a job upon their return, she worked at Pantone as the receptionist. She assumed it would simply be "a temporary gig...until I could get back into fashion." It became her career choice.

As part of her initial responsibilities at Pantone, Lisa entered information from reply cards and sales of swatch cards, by region, into the company's database to discern likenesses in color preference as well as differences. Every PANTONE Publication included a postcard requesting work information: name, industry, job description and comments. While (answering phones and) entering information into the computer, Lisa noticed that many of the replies came from fashion companies. She began to call some of them and talk to designers, not to secure a position for herself, but to gather information and gain a picture of how fashion designers used PANTONE Colors in their work. "It's a great tool to shop Europe, then send the colors off to Asia for manufacturing," they concurred. Uniformly, they also pointed to the color gaps she had noticed while working for the hosiery manufacturer. Still, despite the missing fashion colors, the system provided a means to communicate color internationally.

With the new fashion and interior system Lisa had worked on with Richard in progress, the invaluable input echoed her own notions about the limitations of the PANTONE MATCHING SYSTEM when it came to fashion. Unlike the PANTONE Book for graphic designers, which covered just about every printable color, its tint and shade, textile fashion colors changed seasonally and presented several mixed palettes with accompanying rationales. Knowing that the new system would help confirm Larry's growth objectives, Lisa excitedly brought the news to her father, ready to become a permanent part of the Pantone team.

The 1,800-color palette selected by Al DiBernardo and Mike Garin went through further iterations. Many of the colors were too close for the printing process to control, the method by which this first generation would be produced. The palette needed additional culling. The printing press for the color system laid down seven colors per page, making the optimum number of colors 1,001 for the new system, which meant cutting out almost 700 more colors. Once the final 1,001 colors had been selected, each was assigned a number based on lightness, hue angle and saturation, just as in the original PANTONE MATCHING SYSTEM. The daunting task of naming all 1,001 colors came next.

Reenter Richard. Upon graduating Rensselaer PolyTechnic Institute in 1983, he had joined the company and immediately resumed his work to complete the PANTONE Professional Color System. "It was time to take the research and turn it into a product," Richard explains. Though Larry had originally conceived of Richard's involvement as a summer job that would end when the system had been completed, the Professional Color System would prove to be Richard's first of many projects to come. For Richard, moving from research to actualization became the more interesting part of the process. "I could use my computer background."

Richard bought a computer program from his alma mater, one that, once programmed by him, could convert the plotted colors and match them to the U.S. National Bureau of Standards.[33] He rented an IBM PC, since the hard drive models already on order were eight weeks from delivery, and jumped right in. He began by entering each color's scientific coordinates, known as tristimulus values (three-point coordinates in color space), and then considered the several name options offered by the computer. The National Bureau of Standards/Inter Society Color Council system created explanatory color terms for each of the fifteen hues with modifiers for the degree of brightness or saturation such as light, medium, dark, deep, vivid, pale, -ish (as in yellowish) and so forth.

From Abbey to Zuni Brown, names were assigned to each of the 267 central colors to offer a practical reference as well as a more poetic feel. Entering coordinates for a particular purple color, for instance, prompted names like Pansy Violet, Lavender and Petunia Purple, names that conjure specific color memories.

Over decades, descriptive labels change. "These new names are created for the press and buyers," explains Lee Eiseman. "When you change the name of a color, you evoke a completely new set of

[33] *Color: Universal Language and Dictionary of Names (Special Publication 440, Dec 1976).*

emotions and sensations. Forget your basic orange and green. Ignore purple. Disregard brown and wine. Now you can select from pumpkin, parsley, eggplant, chocolate or claret."

An added consideration for Richard and Lisa, however, was the length of the name. In order to fit on the guide, no name could exceed seventeen characters. One by one, the duo selected names, which Richard's computer program then set aside to avoid any duplication. It didn't take long, however, before they began to run out of designations. Because the majority of the color space coordinates run in the green range, for example, once they passed into the blue-greens, name modifications became necessary. A variation of aqua might end up designated Dusty Aqua.

Once they had finally named all the colors, an interior design consultant reviewed their choices and discussed modifications to accommodate the global marketplace. Though internationally recognizable from a visual viewpoint, the color names had to be translated and understood in six languages: English, Spanish, Italian, French, German and Japanese. That forced the modification of a couple hundred out of the thousand designations. Richard explains, "Barn red, for example, may work in the United States, but its literal translation into, say, Spanish — *granero rojo* — doesn't work. There aren't any red barns in Spain or even Mexico, I don't think." By the time the color naming had finally been turned over to the translation company, they commented that their committee even dreamed in Technicolor.

The subtle-colored palette for apparel and home would sell so well when it hit the U.S. market in late 1984, European marketer, *mode information*, known as specialists in the fashion industry, would join forces with Pantone and help sweep the European fashion designers off their feet. As a result, the American market for this catch-all lifestyle industries system would be left in a bit of a quandary with U.S. fashionistas thinking Pantone originated in Europe. Some even took to pronouncing it 'Pan tó nee' or 'Pan to néh.'

As the system neared completion, Lisa had already secured a position in Pantone's public relations department, remaining close to the project. Larry, in fact, had initiated the idea. 'You know, Lisa, this could be good for you. Why don't you head PR and be our liaison with the PR firm?" Punctuating her reaction with laughter just as Larry might do, Lisa acknowledged the idea as sound and placed herself on Pantone's permanent role call.

Commencing with the Print '85 trade show, held that year in Chicago, Lisa's major goal lay in positioning Pantone as a brand. That meant gathering supporters and loosening Larry's tight grip, even though he had previously revealed his showmanship side.

Lisa ordered a large booth space at Print '85 and, together with the marketing department, helped create a live show. The presentation, the Carousel of Color, called for a production company, actors, scripting and a promo movie shot on a Florida theme park carousel. The trade show's booth and the collateral materials given away at the show expanded the PR budget. But glitzy public relations didn't translate into sales for Larry, the consummate bottom-line guy. "The tangibles were really not there for him, but, at the end of the day, it's all about perception," explains Lisa. "It's not about the bottom line."

Larry would refute this argument. "I understand spending money to promote your name, but what are we doing it for if not to sell product? I know I bought into some of these big-ticket concepts, but the follow-through just wasn't there at the time. Everybody needed to think more practically." Larry's tough love style of guidance initiated, no, forced follow-through strategies that today continue to positively impact the company's sales and profitability.

Ever his willing student, Lisa had set her sights higher. No longer content to be Director of Public Relations, she now wanted to head Corporate Communications in order to strategize advertising and public relations campaigns and work in tandem with the sales and marketing teams to continue to create a brand name.

There was only one way to make that happen. For the first time, Lisa had to devise a logical plan to present to Larry, and she had to do it quickly because the sales department wanted to control corporate communications. At the house in the Hamptons, Lisa worked through the weekend with the aid of a friend from Kirschenbaum & Bond, the well-known advertising agency. Together, they mapped out an umbrella strategy — on paper towels.

At the time, Pantone had run through advertising directors. Larry let one after another go because they were either inadequate or spent too much money. He had finally brought aboard a new agency headed by a friend of his, but he still needed an in-house person. Though he mentioned it to Lisa, she went for the bigger ticket.

That Monday, Lisa took her father to lunch at his favorite Chinese restaurant to soften him up.

"Daddy, I think I should take over Corporate Communications. I have the skills, especially after heading PR."

When she didn't elicit an immediately positive response, she reached into her purse and pulled out the paper towels. Laying the plan on the already cleared table, she began to walk him through her scheme. Though she hadn't intended to show him the actual plan, it seemed like the only way to convince him.

Larry raised his eyes and chuckled. "Well, at least I know you worked over the weekend."

Paper towels notwithstanding, the plan, along with her convinceing argument, gained her the position of Director of Corporate Communications.

Working with Richard, who held the position of vice president of sales and marketing at that time and was technically her boss, and for Larry, still the head of the company, required adroitness on Lisa's part. Plans and ideas had to meet Richard's sales and marketing needs but still pass muster with Larry. Disagreements usually centered on money. Still, Larry was "just a little easier on me because I'm his daughter," Lisa purports. "I think Richard had it a lot harder being responsible for the bottom line."

Lisa's actions eventually triggered a face-off — not with her father but with Richard. When business issues arose in the office, the two could separate apples and oranges, which enabled them to work as teammates and discuss problems with a project. Other times when Lisa would come to Richard for advice, the siblings were not averse to arguing their points. Lisa occasionally took the familial tact. "You're still my little brother," she'd joke. For Richard, the comment reflects Lisa's humor. But Lisa is, in her own way, as doggedly determined as her father and can get things done.

Integrating the PANTONE Professional Color System into a branded product stood high on Lisa's list of goals. First, the System was renamed the PANTONE for Fashion and Home Color System to make a clear distinction from the PANTONE MATCHING SYSTEM for graphics arts, thus improving its market direction. The newly created department soon became an important contributor to the company's bottom line.

Along the way, several textile marketing directors came and went, until one day Richard confronted Lisa. In Larry-esque style he remarked, "Why don't you stop spending the money now and start making the money?" before suggesting that she assume directorship of the division. The awkward manner in which he spoke to Lisa and the backhanded offer reflected both his inexperience as a manager, as well as the fact that he could whack his big sister without repercussion. He would never have taken that tact with anyone else in the company — not Vicky, not even Larry. But Lisa could give as good as she got.

Already somewhat involved in the division on a PR level, the thought of taking over the textile division had never occurred to Lisa. The prospect, once addressed, triggered reflection. "I was good at spending the money," she laughs. "But to finally be responsible for a profit center, build the business, make the money…that was scary. It also meant leaving behind something I loved."

It didn't take long for Lisa to realize that she could still guide a vision and direct a growing area of Pantone's business in her new position — one which would tap her original love of the fashion industry. As senior vice president, textile, home and fashion, Lisa injected the department with just the right amount of drive, dynamism and enthusiasm. With the two at either end of the company holding up the middle, Larry's omnipresence requires a sense of non-interference. But when something goes wrong, "I can talk to anybody around here I want to, but I won't do it in such a way that undermines them. I'm more the inquisitor, but I think that Richard sometimes sees me as the Inquisition-er."

In tandem with their European partner, *mode information*, Pantone converted the original textile system, which had been produced on card stock, to textile swatches — dyed cotton attached to cards. "It was a really important move for the industry to see color on fabric that can be matched in a real-world situation," Lisa points out.

Interior design and furnishing colors have always reflected the times: '40s somber tones spoke of war, '50s lighter pastels drew us back to life, late '60s intense psychedelic neons reflected the radicalism of the times, the '70s saw a return to earth and nature, the '80s gave us flash and dash, while the '90s resurrected black to stand for sophistication and empowerment. Recessions reintroduced neutrals and a better economy spewed bright retro hues. But not until this latest Pantone move did designers have real control over those fashion trends. "The PANTONE Textile Color System, which in 1989 was further enlarged to 1,225 colors in response to continuing and growing customer feedback, gave the fashion and interior designer the power to be the creative force and specify color," Lisa explains. "Before that, they had to resort to the off-the-shelf availability of whatever the mills provided. We really changed that dynamic by providing a comprehensive system. Now designers could direct the mills, 'I love this fabric, but make it in mandarin orange.'"

By providing a universal color language for the fashion, textile, interior and industrial design markets, the PANTONE Textile Color System soon became the *de facto* color standard for the apparel and home textile industries. Decades later, it continues to stand alone as the world's most widely used and recognized color standard. Pantone, however, would not limit itself to either the printing press or the dye vat. The age of technology had dawned.

THE KING *of* COLOR

14

Digitizing Color

Pantone's ability to ride the wave of change, to foresee trends and prepare for them, even roll with the punches when blindsided, had always given it the edge. The age of technology was no exception. Though the dawn of computer graphics inspired many to predict the demise of the mostly paper and ink-based Pantone, the reverse would prove true. In the information age, Pantone secured its market share. The person largely responsible for that was Richard Herbert.

Richard, who began tagging along to work with his father, watching the new Madison Square Garden arena go up girder by girder across the street, never considered a career in the 'printing' business. Likewise, Larry hadn't always considered Richard as Pantone's 'heir apparent.' But when Richard graduated from Rensselaer Polytechnic Institute in 1983 with a degree in management, his plan to work for a renowned computer company like IBM became short-lived. At graduation, Larry caught his son by surprise. "Why don't you come work for me?" his father asked. Had Larry considered Richard's work with computers and computer graphics a benefit to Pantone as it moved into the age of technology? Richard was reticent at first. What he had envisioned for himself lay in the field of computer science. After some discussion, however, mostly coming from Larry, Richard realized that this was an opportunity he shouldn't pass up. Three thoughts entered his mind. Most immediately, the PANTONE Professional Color System needed completion. He could marry two worlds by introducing Pantone to computers. This could be the first step to other possibilities at Pantone — perhaps even taking over some day.

Designers had been "speaking in Pantone" since 1963, well before Silicon Valley provided the tools to move from paper and ink to computer screens and keyboards. Around the same time Richard joined Pantone and resumed his work to complete the PANTONE Professional Color System, later known as the PANTONE Textile Color System, IBM had introduced its first color personal computer, an event that signaled new possibilities for Pantone's expansion. Richard recognized that he could be on the driving end of this technology growth and approached Larry with the proposition to change analog color chips into digital information.

Not since the inception of the PANTONE MATCHING SYSTEM has a concept so aroused the little giant. The two traveled to Silicon Valley to meet with Mindset, a company that launched the first PC-compatible computer with expanded color capability, to put Pantone on the high tech research and development track. Mindset executives sent Richard an IBM PC clone inserted with a video chip that displayed 512 colors. Even while preparing for the Print '85 Show, as well as the launch of the new PANTONE Professional Color System begun years earlier with sister Lisa, Richard turned his attention to researching and learning how the R(ed)G(reen)B(lue) (RGB) system creates color on computers, how monitors display color, and how to stabilize those colors digitally. Every day, he entered his office, turned on the monitor and allowed it to warm up for an hour. He then calibrated the monitor by hand, tuning each gun to ensure color consistency from one day to the next. He plotted his daily calibrations, as well as the color drift of the monitor with a Minolta color meter he had purchased for the job.

Though Pantone ultimately didn't link up with Mindset, Richard and Larry returned with startlingly new information and a heightened awareness of future possibilities. Richard, given his background, had foreseen the future of technology for Pantone. Larry hadn't quite succumbed to the argument. Still, never one to miss a good business opportunity and as a goodwill gesture, he granted Richard free reign to research and develop the RGB database for color display on monitors. This would ultimately lead to Pantone's Electronic Color Systems (ECS) Division, officially launched in 1987 with Richard at the helm and responsible for all technology-based color product development and licensing. Major contentions would also erupt between father and son.

Through sheer determination, Richard had readied a prototype

191

digital system by 1985 that married designers to the computer using PANTONE Colors. He worked in conjunction with a company called Via Video (Network Picture Systems) to develop a proprietary system, one that Pantone would own and license to them, and launched the system, worth $150,000, at the Print '85 Show. Though overhauled later that year aided by the inception of the 386-computer which allowed for a less expensive, more standardized platform for the PANTONE System, the impact Pantone made on design technology thrust them forward.

Richard felt sure that Pantone sat at the forefront of change. The lack of real standards for displays or easy calibration methods, however, impeded the company's progress. Though Pantone led the way, the company still had a long way to go.

The launch of the Apple Macintosh II in 1987 that computerized color publishing unveiled a new reality for Richard's work. Having accomplished the color design program on the PC, he sprang into action and avidly pursued licensing deals with software and hardware makers for his calibrated color system. Each time Richard met with manufacturers to pitch the product, the story offered was routinely the same. With the exception of a few individuals, they all misconstrued the concept and just who would benefit.

"We're going to put your color system in our product and you're going to sell a lot of chips books to people we sell software to," they asserted.

Each time, Richard set the record straight. "We're already selling

PANTONE Books to the people you want to sell to. By putting our colors into the software, you're going to make your product more attractive and useful for a customer that *we already have*. That's why you have to pay us a royalty."

Those royalties based on new technology hardware and software products marketed by Pantone at one point represented fifteen percent of Pantone's revenues and reached nearly thirty percent profit in some years.

Richard orchestrated his very first Macintosh licensing agreement in 1987 with a software company called LaserWare. The company's owner, a transplant from the printing industry, understood the need for tools that designers could be comfortable with — including PANTONE Colors.

Since then, as a result of Richard's ECS (Electronic Color Systems) Division, most desktop publishing programs and color printers now incorporate PANTONE for color. Under his direction, Pantone has licensed major companies in the technology world that issue color-producing products — Microsoft Publisher®, QuarkXPress®, Adobe® Illustrator®, Adobe Photoshop®, Hewlett-Packard, Xerox.

Richard's skyrocketing success helped him set his sites on other goals, namely the presidency which his father occupied. Though the two never openly discussed succession, Richard knew the head spot was attainable and focused on strengthening his professional limitations. His undergraduate degree in management gave him a good base, but he opted to further his education at Hofstra, graduating in 1985 with an MBA in banking and finance. Not until the middle of the next decade, however, would the opportunity for Richard's training present itself and, along with it, a test of wills with his father.

Larry, too, had a banner year by the end of 1987 and through 1988. Despite the economic downturn after five years of boom, Larry felt the same product could not hold up forever without an investment on his part. In the past two decades, the role of color had played a major part in all arenas of design and throughout the world. The Asian and European sensibilities about color differed from the American. None of this came as a surprise to Larry who had originally designed the PANTONE MATCHING SYSTEM with the U.S. market in mind.

As sales of the swatch cards were tracked by region, different colorations popped to the top of the lists between the areas. Though Larry had offered additional tools, the system called for updating, a new version that designers would need and demand.

Pantone technicians began to analyze how to incorporate the desired colors into the system. Though the number of new colors actually required fell to less than 247, in order to fold in the colors in an organized way, Pantone had to incorporate that many. For the first time since the inception of his PANTONE MATCHING SYSTEM, the palette increased from 500 to 747 colors. Launched first in Japan, demand increased. Instead of the usual twice-yearly print run, Pantone now printed and sold three runs of the fan-style color books.

The high margins and additional licensed art materials in new colors helped sales surpass expectations by more than 50 percent, and the new book's sweeping popularity took a full 18 months to fill the pipeline.

Larry used the opportunity to hire an advertising agency and plan two campaigns: one based on the system's 747 colors, the same designation for the Boeing planes that frequently flew to Japan, and the rationale behind its launch there; and the other featuring playing cards and the slogan "If you are not using the 747, you're not playing with a full deck." The campaigns garnered favorable attention and generated blockbuster sales.

When Pantone first launched its "Designer's Choice" tracking system in the 80s, differences in color preference were far more apparent. Though the PANTONE MATCHING SYSTEM has been updated since, today's merchandising phenomenon has become so global that one would be hard-pressed to find real differences in preference.

Letraset, the art supply distributor Larry had licensed in 1972 to produce art materials matching the PANTONE Colors and to sell books, buoyed the sales success of the PANTONE MATCHING SYSTEM even more. To keep abreast with Pantone and support the newest array of colors, they had to increase the volume of materials offered. Their expansion of the entire line — markers, color acetates and papers — inflated Pantone's bottom line since, as Larry proudly reminded whoever would listen, Pantone now made money not only on new book sales but from increased royalties.

This love affair with Letraset lasted only another year. Though Letraset produced artist materials, Pantone took the position that it had the right to produce artists' paints to match the system. Letraset disagreed. Allegedly, there had been an unwritten agreement between the two companies stipulating that Letraset receive the first right of refusal to produce the paints. "We did give them right of first refusal," announced Larry. "Conveniently, they didn't remember it."

In court, Larry stood before Judge Pollack, the very same judge from the Para-Tone case a decade earlier, to listen to the ruling that stated Letraset had the exclusive right to use the PANTONE Trademark for all artist materials, excluding Pantone itself. "He knocked us out of the box," insisted Larry. "That made us incapable of doing business with anybody anymore. I couldn't let that go." Four months later, the Appellate Division reversed the decision with the proviso that any new ideas in the art material category be presented to Letraset for first refusal. Letraset's loss sent the relationship on a downward spiral. New product ideas came with increasing demands from Letraset for Pantone to spend money unnecessarily, on things like market studies. This was the proverbial straw for Larry who had been sabotaged by them some eight years earlier.

At the time, Pantone manufactured the products for Letraset to sell, including the popular fan book. Somehow, Letraset seduced Larry's vice president of finance into supplying them with manufacturing costs which included information on Larry's loans, one of which he covered with future royalty payments from Letraset. Letraset discovered the due date of this note — ten days after receipt of the royalties from them — and held back the money, leaving Larry in a precarious situation with the bank. One of Larry's employees informed him that his finance guy had copied and handed information to Letraset and then followed it up with a formal letter informing Letraset that Pantone officially had fallen into default.

Larry smelled a rat. Armed with his cocktail of wariness and cautiousness on every business front, Larry confronted the bank vice president. "Arthur, how could they have found out that I secured this loan based on receipt of royalties?" he asked rhetorically.

No answer.

"Because, as I figure it, the only way it could have come out is from this office. The only way they could have known is from you," blurted Larry.

Larry felt, but couldn't prove at the moment, that the President of Letraset America had been in on the scheme. Nevertheless, vengeance would have to wait. He didn't have time to play Sherlock, he had his company to resurrect. Completely tapped, he turned to someone he knew, a businessman introduced to him by his attorney, who agreed to loan him the $400,000 at 25 percent interest, with Larry's fully paid co-op as collateral. He cleared his loan with the bank, received his royalty money from Letraset, paid the businessman the $400,000 plus a couple thousand for a few days' use.

Then Larry cleaned house. Out went anyone associated with the conspiracy. The bank's vice president was fired, as was the President of Letraset America. When the head of the Letraset Corporation came to New York from England, Larry accepted his invitation to lunch, after which he questioned him. "John, did you know what was going on?" To which John replied, "Yeah, but I wouldn't have handled it the way they did."

"Too bad, John, we've known each other for many years. You see what happens when I'm wronged. You were supposed to be a friend," replied Larry as he stood up and walked out of the restaurant.

Richard, in the meantime, continued his work on the newest iteration of color software and introduced the new program to the graphic arts community in 1990.

He called it the PANTONE Professional Color Toolkit. Co-developed by Pantone and Radius (who developed an automated monitor calibrator), this piece of code delivered accurate PANTONE Colors to the Radius display.

Digital colors (computers and television) work on an entirely different color system from pigments — paints, inks and dyes. Instead of blue, red and yellow (CMYK: Cyan, Magenta, Yellow and Black for printing purposes), the light transmitting system is based on red, green and blue (RGB). Each color makes up a pixel (short for picture element), sometimes called dots. To achieve the 256 available colors, percentages of light of these three colors are added to a black screen,

MONITORING COLOR

*The number of bits (binary digit, a unit of information)
used to represent each pixel determines how many colors
or shades of gray can be displayed. For example, 1 bit is
monochrome; in 8-bit color mode, the color monitor
uses 8 bits for each pixel, making it possible to display
two to the 8th power, or 256, different colors or shades
of gray; a 24 to 32 bit graphic represents true color.*

which is why the system is referred to as "additive." If 100 percent light transmission of each color is achieved, the result is pure white. Millions of these pixels arranged in rows and columns close together form the graphic on the screen. A close eyeball inspection of a computer monitor will show the points on the screen.

The PANTONE Professional Color Toolkit also became a central piece of code that any other licensee could tap into. The inherent problem with digital color started with monitor calibration — or lack of it — to a known standard or white balance. For instance, TV broadcast standards rely on the NTSC guidelines. Graphic designers had no such standards. If a monitor isn't color calibrated to a known standard or profiled to specific conditions or use, the resulting color could be off, just as it was when Larry began solving the matching problem with printed color.

Not only do people see colors differently, the devices they use —
monitors, scanners and printers — see them differently as well.
Designer Milton Glaser explained the problem in terms of mediums
used and other variables. "…you get things like the surface you are
working on, the humidity, the light that you are viewing work in. One
of the great problems is the transformation from a computer screen
to a flat piece of paper. You are talking about trying to duplicate something that exists under dramatically different conditions. The computer image with light source behind it is different than something
that appears on a piece of paper."

A second, more recent problem occurred with the growth of digital photography. When the camera translates the energy it captures
(the image) into RGB color space, certain areas of color space are not
well defined. For example, let's say you photograph a purple subject.
When you look at it on an LCD screen, the purple object might
appear turquoise or a light blue. When downloading, if the monitor
is not calibrated, the image comes through from one set of RGBs to
another set of RGBs, and the color will ultimately look different. It's
like trying to match American English to the Queen's English. It's the
same language, only it comes out differently. Furthering the problem
of an uncalibrated monitor is the translation of RGB color space (the
monitor), a triangular shape, into print or CMYK pentagram-shaped
color space (the printer). Triangles to pentagrams: round pegs, square
holes.

With the different color space mediums, translating what

appears on the screen to a printer can be stupefying, which is one of the reasons Pantone created Hexachrome®, a patented six-color printing system (CMYK plus Green and Orange). Again, each pixel, or point, is composed of red, green and blue. Ideally, the three colors, when emitted, should all converge at the same point. When they do not, it generally means that the monitor is not correctly calibrated, leaving a fuzzy appearance. The real world cannot be captured in the digital environment without compression. An image changes even more from digital camera to monitor as it shrinks again and changes shape. By the time the image hits the printer, it barely resembles the original colors. The once glorious sunset has lost its glow because it is outside the color range or gamut of your devices. The image has been compromised. Furthering the dilemma is the fact that gamut clipping (compression) only goes in one direction. It can never go backwards.

Our eyes capture and reproduce more of the real world, and though many colors may reproduce well on a monitor, by the time you reach CMYK printing, you have shrunk to a much smaller range. Color management tries to preserve the integrity of the image through mathematics. It won't give you the exact color but will maintain color balance and contrast. So, greens will remain green, just not as perfectly as your eyes recall. Perhaps this is not a concern when it comes to home photos, but when triple digit millions of dollars are spent on packaging, advertising, promotion and point of purchase displays, the manufacturer has a greater stake in color achievement.

Hexachrome printing betters the chance of a one-to-one translation: screen to printer. Any output device needs to be profiled, whether CMYK, Hexachrome or inkjets, with a good color gamut in order to translate from one to another. The deficiency is not necessarily in the technology as much as in the implementation of the right calibration and profiling from origination to destination. Hexachrome can match over 90 percent of the spot colors found in the PANTONE formula guide (as opposed to 50 percent in four-color printing), providing richness, depth and range; making the Disney characters on the Kellogg's cereal boxes look as child-appealing .as in the original movies. The only issue left to tackle remains the fundamental physical problem of transmitted color versus reflected color. Unless science can find a way to calibrate the human eye, there will always be some variation.

Pantone's business began to take on a new look as it ventured into a new era — from the exclusively paper and print supported concern held closely by Larry to an amalgamation which included Richard's digital enterprises. The timing could not have been better. Had the digital business not emerged when it did, the company would have suffered from the 1990 recession, as well as from its soured relationship with Letraset that resulted in an overstock of books. As analog licensing sales numbers stagnated, the digital business took up the slack. That, as Richard who graphed the company's income puts it, "saved our ass."

Ironically, the ECS Division, only six strong, was organized and run as though a totally separate entity. Larry, who suited up every day, had rules about appearance and promptness. Casually dressed, Richard and his team worked downstairs and apart from the others. They even had their own PR firm. For Richard, working in the area of technology felt akin to being in Silicon Valley where he had seen people show up at work in jeans, make their own hours, even roller-blade through the hallways.

Not surprisingly, Richard's laid back attitude regarding attire laid down by Larry led to resentment among other Pantone workers and a test of wills with Larry. To add to the mix, while Richard ran the software development division downstairs, he and his programmers decided to forego things like the general lunchroom coffee upstairs and make their own. They set up a coffee pot in the back room of the Electronic Color Systems Division. This only added to the grumblings about special privilege until coffee grounds were found on the floor and the matter brought to Larry's attention. He found this renegade behavior typical of the department and demanded the coffee pot removed.

The mutinous protests struck Larry like a knife as he confronted Richard in the boardroom. Since Richard's arrival at Pantone, father and son had undergone typical business problems since they didn't always see eye-to-eye. But in Larry's mind, ECS wasn't clearly defined in terms of the individual tasks or accomplishments. Discussions ensued surrounding "paying a person to do a job" versus "paying someone to be at work on time." Larry required that the crew of six punch a time clock like some others did. In his view "they acted like a bunch of spoiled kids" and needed to be reined in. Larry and Richard squared off. Richard brought up the one-size-fits-all employee policy under which Pantone had been run, regardless of pay scale or position. He pointed to the need for a more aggressive pay scale to attract and retain skilled personnel to his division, an area that would move the company into the future. Without it they would experience continual turnovers. The discussion heated between the two as onlookers sat in silence. Larry would have none of this nonsense — one set of rules for Richard's group and another for everyone else. Regardless of the business advances made by Richard, Larry still called the shots. Period!

Concerned about the results over the past few years, Larry conferred with Richard, seeking advice on recruiting a replacement, or just maybe he deliberately planted a seed that took.

"Look, Dad, before you hire anybody else, let me take over the sales end of it," Richard quickly replied. "I couldn't do worse than the people you've had."

After just fifteen minutes of thought, Larry accepted Richard's proposition.

Once established in sales, Richard immersed himself in marketing and merged the two operations, moving himself into the position of vice president of sales and marketing. "I knew it was a necessary stepping stone to become president," Richard philosophizes. "I needed the sales and marketing experience as part of my leadership training." Richard couldn't have known at this time, but his goal to attain the presidency was nearly assured.

Though Richard realized he could potentially step into the presidency, he also knew that he had to prove his worth. Before throwing himself into sales and marketing, he had worked on what would become one of Pantone's most important technical developments. Begun in 1991 amidst the company turmoil, the initiative to find a better standard for printing came together. Called the Hi-Fi Project, it assembled leaders from all aspects of the printing industry — ink manufacturers, software programmers, hardware makers and commercial presses. Progressive printers at this time had already tuned to six-, eight- and ten-color presses, but these lacked a certain efficiency.

"We already knew that when you base your colors on the four-color process," declares Richard, "you could only reproduce about 50 percent of the PANTONE Color Range. My father has known this for decades. So why not create a system that could have more depth and scope than four-color process?"

To support the project, each company worked in its particular area of expertise in search of a solution: Agfa worked on imaging with new screening technology (to eliminate conflicting dot patterns called moirés); Aldus, now part of Adobe, ran the area of page layout and color management; Kodak controlled the area of automated color separation technology (to separate an image into more than four colors in an automated way). And, of course, Pantone, in competition with Dupont, worked on actual color systems.

The system had to be an integrated six-color system, not a four-color process with, say, orange added on when and where needed. "If you build a flesh tone in four-color process, you could scientifically create it with yellow and magenta and some added black or cyan, in some cases," explains Richard. "In six-color, you would always formulate it with yellow, orange and magenta, and then black, giving better color range, better balance and the ability to achieve more accurate ethnicities, for example."

Dupont initially devised a system called Hyper Color: combining four colors plus bumps of cyan, magenta and yellow. This increased the range but required a base of seven colors. Growing sales of six-color printing presses fueled Pantone's approach to the solution. How could six colors be standardized?

Richard, like Larry, worked as a hands-on inventor. While testing the ink combinations on press, Richard would push them to maximum density. Trial and error? "Not in terms of the colors," according to Richard. "From a scientific point of view, we already knew where the colors had to come from, but until we saw actual results, we were never really sure."

The new palette updated cyan, magenta and yellow from the original standard, added black for shading, and a particular orange and green to make six colors.

BLUE FUNK

*Cyan blue, originally extracted from cornflower petals
and known as cornflower blue, was replaced by a
synthetic version in the late nineteenth century derived
from the poisonous chemical cyanide. Causing death
to dye workers, the color, as well as use of the name, was
discontinued until the advent of color photography.*

To vitalize the colors and give them a high-octane appearance, Richard added fluorescence, an integral part of Pantone's new Hexachrome Color System patent. The integrated six-color system rendered a more realistic direct match not only to the PANTONE Colors but also to the dynamic range of Ektachrome film used predominately by professionals at that time. Unfortunately, the Hexachrome print process had only slowly been adopted by printers, most unwilling to trade up to newer technology and machinery. The revolution came with computer to plate (CtP) work warranting software to split an image into the Hexachrome colors for printing with conventional screens, angles or stochastic screen. HexWare® software helped reinstate Pantone as a player in the fast-growing technology field by supporting Abobe Photoshop and Adobe Illustrator used by designers and prepress preparation and printers

THE STOCHASTIC SCREEN

The stochastic screen was invented in the 1930s by Alexander Murray. It is a random dot-patterned screen or grid used in printing to eliminate linear or moiré patterns annoying to the eye.

who worked in the large gamut, six-color Hexachrome process.

Generally, working on a computer screen meant compromise when it came to the four-color printing. With Hexachrome, there is less color compromise. "It's a 'what you see is what you get' type of approach," according to Richard.

With the insets locked down and Kodak's separation engine in place, Pantone went to press with the accompanying color guide which presented the range of colors. "That's what Pantone does best," says Richard. The system, completed in 1994, made its official launch in the spring of 1995 at the DRUPA international print show in Germany and earned Richard a co-patent for its invention.

The original Hi-Fi Initiative became the Pantone initiative, and Hexachrome and its subsequent color technologies stretched the field from design to printing. Both produced by Pantone and licensed out, Pantone's technologies standardized digital color and remain to this day inexpensively supported by QuarkXPress, CorelDRAW®,

Macromedia Freehand® and offered plug-ins for Adobe Illustrator and Adobe Photoshop. All the major profiling tools supported Hexachrome.

Richard rationalized his initial involvement in the Hi-Fi program as part of his resolve for Pantone's future to become part of the leading edge of graphic arts technology. Moreover, he realized that any Hi-Fi initiative-evolved colors could readily compete with Pantone and that this new technology could threaten business. His philosophy: "Why not let it come from us? Let Pantone control the new color options."

Richard perceived his challenge as achieving greater adoption of the digital technology: getting more printers to use it and designers to specify it. He still does. Like the innovative PANTONE MATCHING SYSTEM that preceded it three decades earlier, the cost of entry included anyone who wanted to buy the system.

Richard didn't stop there. Internet-safe colors for Web applications debuted in 1996 with PANTONE Colorweb®, a way to select PANTONE Colors from within favorite applications and apply the right HTML values.

Often labeled a monopoly, the fact that Pantone's dominance now expands throughout the digital world tickles the company's founder. A popular solution for retail packaging and advertising, Hexachrome had rarely, if ever, been used for an entire book before Harvard University Press published *The Smaller Majority* in 2005. When accomplished digital photographer and Director of the

Invertebrate Diversity Initiative at Harvard University's Museum of Comparative Zoology, Piotr Naskrecki, agreed to publish his book with Harvard University Press, they investigated color printing processes and sources. Nearby DS Graphics in Lowell, MA, printed a press proof of eleven of Dr. Naskrecki's photographs without color correction, showing four-color and Hexachrome side by side. The wider range of color and added depth of Hexachrome were immediately apparent. As work on the book began, DS Graphics converted native RGB files to Hexachrome, created low-resolution files for Harvard's designer to lay out the pages in QuarkXPress, then upgraded its Fuji contract proofing system for Hexachrome.[34]

Similarly, Odwalla Inc., the producer of all-natural pure squeezed, pure pressed fruit and vegetable juices, had its labels converted into Hexachrome. "We converted all of Odwalla's spot color artwork to Hexachrome using Pantone's Hexware software," related Roman Artz, national account manager at Inland Printing, Dixie Printing & Packaging adopted Hexachrome because it was looking for greater efficiency. With Hexachrome, they could gang their products and run them together instead of using 20 spot colors. Even movie/production studios, like Disney, use Pantone to keep their cartoon characters clothes and body parts color-consistent. "We've been called the color mafia," laughs Larry, still a vigorous and involved character whose unlined face and energetic form belie his septuagenarian-plus years.

[34] *http://www.pantone.com/articles/pdfs/art_ElectronicPublication_Hex1205.pdf*

The first mover into color space, Pantone not only created a language but also marketed its brand so widely and so effectively that not even the world's largest technology company could compete. Microsoft, who had tried to produce an imbedded color coding system of its own, eventually realized the need for consistency which the PANTONE Language provided and took a license from Pantone for its Microsoft Publisher software.

"Microsoft and Kodak both tried to compete with us by developing a color management solution," Larry gloats. "You would think that Kodak and Microsoft getting together would be able to sink Pantone. But the point is: How many Oxford dictionaries do you have in your house?"

THE KING *of* COLOR

15

Ascending the Rainbow Throne

Business flourished during the second half of the '90s mostly due to Richard's technology acumen and comprehensive understanding of Pantone's markets. Building product for digital technology based on the Pantone philosophy made sense. Richard was itching to move forward. He had big, important goals, including a vision of a consumer-oriented retail environment for color. With numerous innovations and increased sales under his belt, he positioned himself to take over the presidency, but the reluctant and powerful Larry would not be moved out so easily.

Although the ambitious, younger Herbert may never have directly Said 'I want to be president' to his father, by 2000, with maturity on his side, he felt the time had come for his father to consider a succession plan. Moreover, he clearly saw himself as the heir apparent. As far as he was concerned, he had made all the right moves. His father had always said he respected others who worked toward a goal and grabbed what they wanted, as opposed to those who just sat back waiting to be asked. So Richard had proceeded with this in mind. He had realized the digital side of the business, which was now responsible for a rising percentage of the company's profit and growth; he had obtained an MBA without fatherly prodding; and had run sales and marketing.

"Could I have ultimately become president by staying on the technology side of the business? Probably," contends Richard. "But the additional knowledge I gleaned in sales and marketing, as well as in business school, gave me an edge." Certainly, Richard's track record primed him as executive vice president under Larry, but that wasn't the point. "Isn't the natural progression for a son who works for his father to some day take over the business?" he explained.

Well before his appointment as president, the times called for change. Since his remarriage in 1986, Larry had begun to spend less time at the Carlstadt, New Jersey, office and more time with his new family. That only exacerbated an organizational problem at the ever-growing Pantone. Perhaps because Larry had been the sole person with his finger in every pie, each department had worked nearly as a separate entity for years. Walls kept projects created in one realm secretive until they were tossed like grenades over the wall into the next arena. The sense of sharing projects had not come to fruition until new people entered the scene to properly balance the tasks between intuiters, feelers and doers. Many of the daily details of running the business fell squarely on Richard's shoulders.

Pantone, the color company once solely associated with printing and governed exclusively by Larry Herbert's iron will, steered toward a mixed media future and a flurry of Herbert commanders who all too readily bumped heads.

The company was changing and Pantone needed a new vision. Lisa pointed to Richard for new leadership. "It just made sense." Maintaining Pantone as a thriving family business warranted a solution, and Richard felt sure that he met the criteria.

Lisa, who had worked at Pantone the longest of the siblings, supported his bid for the presidency. Years earlier while at Pantone's Moonachie, New Jersey, location, she had even overheard her father commenting over the phone that "one of these days Richard will grow up to become president of the company." Though she never aspired to the position, Larry admits that Lisa has what Larry refers to as "drive, guts, hunger." Nevertheless, when Richard voiced his desire, Lisa backed him in his quest.

"Well, I think from the day I came here…my goal would be to succeed my father," Richard admits. Although he had worked energetically to acquire the skills needed to become president, Larry remained reluctant to step aside. He needed coaxing. Considered the 'mommy' type of the three and fiercely protective of her little brother, Lisa intervened on Richard's behalf in a most unexpected way.

Through a chance discussion at dinner one evening with a family friend and her entrepreneurial son, she leaned about industrial psychologists. The young entrepreneur explained how he had hired one to help him meld a traditional company with a newly-organized dot com. Intrigued, she found the idea worthy of exploration — an industrial psychologist that specialized in succession planning might help with the transition.

Several people interviewed to work with Pantone on the succession issue, but Lisa wanted someone she thought could grasp the issues and control the people involved. Whoever they hired would have to build a rapport with Larry and gain his respect. Larry was not stupid, and he was no pushover. According to Lisa, "It had to be…like a guy that could relate to LH." The management consultant and psychologist with whom her friend's son had worked, Steven Berglas, Ph.D., fit the bill. Further, Lisa had read an article in *Inc.* magazine by Berglas. In it, he reported on the phenomenon of Pyrrhic Revenge, when one sibling is passed over for another to head a company and becomes destructive. "We didn't have any of that," replied Lisa. "We all felt that Richard should take the lead. And it wasn't about getting Larry out, we just had to get him on board." She presented the information to Richard. "Maybe this would be a good guy to bring in to help," she told her brother. Lisa, Richard and Juergen "Jerry" Stolt, executive vice president, sales & marketing, presented Larry with the prospect.

He knew the topic of succession would rear up one day. Avoiding the issue could be disastrous for the future of Pantone. The problem lay in the fact that Richard wanted to take over now because, as he put it, "Larry was already operating as Chairman, not as President and CEO. It was time for me to graduate to the next step, take on full operational control while he's still here and active in the business so I can benefit from his insight."

Larry had previously consulted an organizational consultant when manufacturing had run amuck. At the time, there appeared to be too many chiefs and not enough productivity, and Larry felt the need to shore up the cracks. Once those issues had been resolved, the consultant continued to provide insight into the sales and marketing area. "We had to function better," remarks Richard. "Every company has its level of dysfunctionality. For us, because the company grew up in various ways and at different speeds, — we had the printing side, the textile side and the ECS side — there were multiple cultures and mindsets. Yet the leadership was autocratic. We just weren't running like one of my father's presses, a well-oiled machine."

During the period before his bid for the presidency, while holding much of the responsibility, management of the company appeared schizophrenic. Larry and Richard had created a logjam when it came to decisions. Sometimes it was Larry's way, and other times it was Richard's. Moreover, employees felt the strain between the present and the future and, the disparate views, at some point, drew out loyalists on either side.

In the end, Berglas could determine if Richard should move into the presidency and that he could help Larry with the transition. He would not only effectively reorganize Pantone's staffing, his efforts would ultimately help raise Richard's position and power in the company. Larry had marked his future with the first check he issued to the psychologist.

For the next six months, Steve combed through the ranks, interviewing company personnel. He ran classes and pinpointed where the problems lay. He spoke with Larry and conferred with Richard. He then brought the two together. Larry jumped in.

"I need to find out if Richard is going to be capable of running this business or not," he announced bluntly.

"One of the problems, Larry, is that Richard feels he should have more authority," explained Steve Berglas. "And he doesn't want to wait for you to die to get it."

"Well, that's okay with me," responded Larry, "provided he can handle the job."

Larry then turned to Richard with these words. "You want to be president of this company? You've got to make decisions. Tough and sometimes unpopular, but you've got to make them."

Torn by the pressure to relinquish his position, Larry understood the necessity to develop a viable succession plan to keep the company within the family. Still he hesitated to step down. This dichotomy emerged when it was realized that Larry had educated and groomed Richard all along.

As a member of the American Film Institute, a restorer of old films, Larry traveled to Los Angeles for meetings. When A.F.I. instituted its digital lab, Richard accompanied Larry to see the new technology. They traveled to Japan to work with distributors, and back in the U.S. they attended trade shows together. If Richard decided to attend a show that Larry hadn't planned to go to, the latter would change his plans and accompany Richard. "I wanted to keep myself informed for one thing, but I also wanted to see how he reacted to the new technologies, what he thought was important and what he thought wasn't."

It wasn't the first time Larry had failed to appreciate Richard's capability. "I think that if I had not asked for the v.p. of sales and marketing job when I did, he would have promoted someone from within the department who would have been less qualified," Richard recalls. "On the other hand, I think he also realized that the sales position would add to my breadth of experience. That's just how my father works —he's sometimes a contradiction in terms."

Changes instituted by Richard in the sales and marketing depart-ment, however, had not always matched Larry's standards. Larry's Pantone ran mostly as a business-to-business operation. "During his heyday," reports Richard, "we never had a field sales force. We had hired a few in-house salesmen who handled non-distributor accounts, paid them whether they succeeded or failed, and if they failed too many times in a row, they were fired."

The job of selling Pantone's product was different then. Over 20 years prior, Larry had a distributorship agreement with Letraset to be his exclusive dealer. Letraset received skids of product into its New Jersey warehouse and shipped to accounts around the world. Pantone's job pretty much ended there, with Letraset handling all advertising and marketing of the product.

But no more. Letraset had been sold and marginalized by the new parent company, Esselte. Now Pantone was selling its own ever-expanding product line through its own sales force. The job's newly expanded responsibilities required a commensurate modification in compensation, one that Larry balked at. With a full sales team in place under Richard's direction, father and son squared off every earnings quarter because Larry had to sign bonus checks for the salespeople.

In those months and weeks leading up to Richard's assuming the presidency of Pantone, Larry would keep his son on edge, at times leading Richard to question himself. At best, the transition coursed a bumpy road.

Larry Herbert, Steve Berglas and Richard met in Richard's office in December of 2000. The last matter at hand: finalizing Richard's appointment so that he could begin his presidency January 2001. The informality of the proceedings left Richard wondering whether the transition was a done deal or just more talk. During the meeting, Larry unceremoniously stated that Richard would take over the presidency come 2001 and ended the meeting without so much as a memo circulated to employees. As Richard's appointment would not be the only position change, a state of the company meeting held for employees soon after announced the changes.

Finally charged with responsibility for the company, Richard began to hire his support team as Larry looked on. "Well, I watched the situation, and I figured the only way people learn is by making mistakes," Larry recalls. "You know, you can tell a child 'Don't touch. It's hot.' But, they don't believe it until they find out for themselves."

"To this day it's a battle," declares Richard. "Times change. The economy changes. To grow profit ten percent annually, you have to increase sales exponentially. Our sales force receives a base rate of pay and bonuses. In a great year, like 2004, we had to pay a ton of bonuses. LH hated doing that. Even when I would point out 'You know what that means? It means you had a great year,' he still thinks the product sells itself and that these guys are going on a free ride. And you know what? I can't change him. All I can do is stay on track, grow the company, do better and better and, hopefully, he'll be satisfied."

Onlookers remark that the pass-off from Larry to Richard went a lot more smoothly than they anticipated. Larry's autocratic style consisted of strong managers who took direction very well. Richard prefers strong managers who dare to contend that "the emperor has no clothes."

Both work from strong cores and gain the same results through different management styles. When Larry hired people, he put them through the paces and they grew into their positions. Richard seeks to recruit individuals who have proven themselves in their respective fields. In Pantone's infancy, Larry had only a few key managers and product shipped through a distributor. There was no IT interface to manage, no human resource group, online shopping store or other divisions to run. If something had to be done, Larry could get up from behind his desk and do it. He had the skills and competency. Richard contends that Larry fails to admit to the company's complexities, that leadership today requires entrusting his divisional vice presidents, something that once had badly burned Larry.

Still, father and son are more alike than not. Both men respond positively to committed personnel. When new ideas come up or problems arise, they will sit and listen. In the history of Pantone, no one has ever been fired for anything frivolous. Both leaders have high expectations of their staff, will challenge them and reward them for doing well. When Ken Niepokoy came up with the idea for the Color Cue®, a small instrument which when laid on a color can match it to a PANTONE Number, the vision came to fruition. When Marketing Vice President Doris Brown had an idea to combine two products into one, she sat with Richard, explored the possibilities, received a "Great idea!" and has since engaged with design company IDEO.

The work environment has relaxed somewhat, but even on dress-down Fridays certain garb is unacceptable: torn jeans, taped-up sneakers and sloppy clothes don't sit well with Larry. The culture varies depending on the work being performed. Pressmen still punch a time clock. Whereas others move about as required.

Richard has learned to handle Larry's harsh stance. Once always in defensive mode, Richard now prefers to sit and clarify the situation in his mind. Though presented to him in terms of black and white, Richard has learned about balance and assuming responsibility. He understands Larry's point about staying on top of his people but also knows that he can't drown in what they are doing on a daily basis.

With over twenty years under his belt, Richard has reminded Larry that aside from the formula guide, the new technologies and allied accomplishments constitute the business. Larry had always contended that risk was necessary, an important part of growing the business, that Richard could not simply act as company custodian behind his desk. While some projects have not gone as Richard had planned, Larry can't have it both ways, informs Richard. Ultimately, they manage to have the same goals but in different time warps.

Their public personas are as different as their professional ones. Unlike Larry, Richard prefers to stay out of the limelight, though aware of the importance of personal PR as president. Owning up to a more reserved nature and camera shy, he admits that Lisa undertakes public speaking and interviews far better than he. He also feels that time doesn't allow for an excess of such things, so the PR department only directs high-level interviews his way.

"He knows that I'm doing the right things. I know he knows. But he still has that battle with me, to keep me on my toes, and I think it is the old guard versus the new...and the fact that I'm his son."

Studies with regard to family succession point out that there is a concerted "lack of willingness of the older generation to 'let go' of ownership and management power."[35] This is not news to Larry who

---

[35] *Birley, Sue. Attitudes of owner-managers' children towards family and business issues; Entrepreneurship: Theory and Practice 26.3, Spring 2002; p5 (15); Baylor University. Quotes from a study by Lank (2000), p 195.*

likes to cite an earlier *Wall Street Journal* study that indicates only 25 percent of the sons of CEOs who take over the position make it in the business. Larry expressly wanted Richard to know that his position was not "a shoe-in situation," Larry's way of advising Richard to work harder and smarter.

Favoring Richard's position, a separate study "examines the differences between founder-controlled firms and firms controlled by descendants or relatives of the founder. In general…founder-controlled firms grow faster and invest more in capital assets and research and development. However, descendant-controlled firms are more profitable. The early years are characterized by rapid growth. The experience of the early years provides a basis for later when the firm is more professionally run and can exploit its established position in the market."[36]

All that means little to Larry, or to onlookers with vested interests. Larry's concerns about Richard's management style were the telltale numbers.

When Pantone's profits began to decline just six months after his promotion, certain that he alone watched the sales reports, Larry voiced his concern to Richard. Whether Richard had been left with a built-up inventory or whether poor sales planning tied up too much money was unclear. For certain, though, Pantone had begun to dab-

---

[36] *Founders versus Descendants: The Profitability, Efficiency, Growth Characteristics and Financing in Large, Public, Founding-Family-Controlled Firms. Daniel L. McConaughy, G Michael Phillips and Kenneth Kaye. Family Business Review 12.2 (June 1999): p123.*

ble in areas previously unknown to them, and in the process had lost focus of the core business.

By the time the devastation of September 11, 2001, rolled around, Pantone's business, in Larry's estimation, could not go further south. He called a meeting to find out what was happening to his once vital company. Larry bellowed, "What the hell are you going to do to pull the year out? Here it is the middle of November. We've got six weeks to go before the end of the year. These decisions should have been made in April." Then he stormed out of the meeting, returned to his office and fumed.

Larry waited for some sort of changes to be made. November passed and he waited. December wrapped up and he waited for someone to act. As January took hold, he finally barreled into Richard's office. "Cut your payroll ten percent and do it this week," he commanded. "End of story." Richard understood. As usual, his father's teaching method had been old school but undeniably clear. Larry expected decisiveness. So he pushed to affect change — maybe too hard or in the wrong way. Larry admits, "I'm still his dad even if we don't always see eye-to-eye on things, and I want to see him succeed, but I am also still responsible for this business."

Richard challenges his father's sense of his business struggle in 2001 and points out that no losses have occurred since he took charge, not only as president, but also since mid-1995 as head of sales and marketing.

Though his father cannot claim the growth of certain newer

business areas, he can claim that everything resulted from his original invention, his business. Larry's work has clearly been remarkable, but many people, the Herbert children included, have contributed to the company's ultimate success.

While Richard waits for the ground to even out, he continues to head a company that, in his estimation, has survived the corporate transition as well as unexpected national setbacks in impressive style. When countless companies showed losses or went out of business in the wake of 9/11, Pantone still made money, just not as much as they had been accustomed to. "Over its lifetime," Richard proudly boasts, "I think you could say that Pantone has been consistently profitable. By most company comparisons, our net income has been pretty strong."

Still, Larry questions every action, examines every detail and suspects every penny spent. At seventy-plus years, he still drives a hard bargain. He still finds it difficult to accept that Pantone must increasingly spend money to make money. To design and institute an aggressive marketing plan costs money. More every year. That doesn't sit well with Larry who still holds the purse strings he has controlled since he acquired Pantone in 1962. "It's a battle every year — to this day — to increase the budget," complains Richard.

"It would have been a battle regardless of who ran the company," Richard admits. "With expansion comes pressure and headaches, and to do things the way they were done back in the early 60s just doesn't work any more." Though seemingly laid back to Larry,

Richard fights a tougher battle than most. While anyone else in his position would certainly have had the same battles with Larry, Richard must tow the line between challenging his father and acceding to his wishes, even against his better judgment.

To promote his Hexachrome system, for example, Richard had planned to FedEx the Colorsuite® for Hexachrome — which included HexWare, a color separation software for Adobe Photoshop and Adobe Illustrator, and color reference guides essential to working in the large gamut, six-color Hexachrome process, as well as Hexachrome test forms and test CD — to the CEOs of the top fifty printing companies in the United States. Despite its $1,000 retail price, the cost of the item was borne by the software's development. "If they see a $1,000 product lying on their desks, given to them for free, with a letter from me asking them to try it, it would have had a tremendous impact at a very low cost," Richard recalls.

This idea actually followed Larry's original line of thinking — if key people use the product, everyone else would follow suit. But Larry felt that a letter alone could do the job. He responded adamantly. "I wrote a letter in 1963 to 21 printing companies [and got 20 positive responses]. Let me write a letter, coming from me personally, to these 50 top CEOs."

Richard didn't think his father's plan would work. "We needed something bigger, more dramatic, more daring. What worked well back in the '60s and even the '70s makes no impact in today's day and age of so much noise. Still, he entertained his father's plan to appease him.

Larry worked with the vice president of marketing to fashion the letter which asked the CEO of the printing company to call Larry, at which point he would follow up by sending the software. The success of his 1963 letter introducing the PANTONE MATCHING SYSTEM was not duplicated. Not one of the 50 printing companies responded to the Hexachrome letter.

"That's how things have changed," Richard says. "CEOs get letters from people all day long. I get letters from people all day long, and I don't respond."

Larry insisted that any interest in the product would have prompted a response and request for a sample. Further, Larry felt that Richard's attitude toward the mailing's failure — it didn't work because my father wouldn't let me do it my way — allows Richard to take the onus off himself. "That's okay," chuckles Larry. "I don't have to be right all the time, just enough of the times."

Laying blame has never washed well with Larry. Directness and answers remain his mode of operation. Lisa's approach always has an ear. She moves about the floor from one end to the other, Richard to Larry. She is as comfortable arguing with Richard about promotional money she needs as she is with Larry to get what she wants. A player, she moves much like Larry to get answers.

Larry knows that Lisa gets away with more than anyone else. Richard's greatest complaint has to do with Lisa spending too much money, for which she doesn't present a plan, get approval for or account for. That had also been Larry's main complaint when it came to Lisa's performance.

Larry may be sticking around, but Richard remains firmly in charge and is carving out his own way of doing business. During one review period, Lisa presented Richard with a list of her accomplishments and future goals, then she had to rank her performance from one to five, where five is the highest rank. This particular year, she and a co-worker had forged a valuable deal with a multi-billion dollar chemical dye company in Switzerland to create a new system. The co-worker rated his performance as a five because the deal had been closed. Lisa rated herself as a four because she tends to be harder on herself, and the work had not progressed as quickly as planned. Despite the fact that she flew to Switzerland twice — once during a blizzard to meet key personnel and put them at ease and another time to proceed with the deal — she believes Richard would probably rate her as a three because the monetary value had not yet been realized. It's a case of 'like father, like son', black and white and no gray: long-term possibilities versus short-term bottom line.

"I don't think they [Larry and Richard] really understand the textile industry and the impact of what this can do for the division," remarks Lisa. The program added some thirty key production companies around the world that can provide in-plant expertise. So, when Gap or Abercrombie & Fitch or any major company produces in India, China or wherever, problems encountered with matching a PANTONE Color can be resolved by one of their technicians who will travel to the factory. Lisa perceives this as a major move in the right direction for Pantone. Start-up costs of creating a program like this on their own would be prohibitive, and now they receive built-in expertise with far reaching tentacles. She bemoans the fact that the head of sales still refers to the textile division as speculative. "Thirty percent to the bottom line is not speculative," she declares. "That's not chopped liver!" Still, she wonders why Richard sees things differently because he is forced to deal with the bottom line as President. "I think back to when we had so much fun, when he was building the ECS Division and we traveled to California. It was all new then, selling the digital color concept, getting the deals. Richard was great at selling a concept, as I did with this. It's hard to find a balance."

The family triangulation allows certain chains of command to be broken. Whether intentional of not, Lisa can get away with sidestepping. Richard rationalizes that as an owner of the company herself, and the owner's daughter, she takes liberties that other employees in her position could not or would not take. Somewhat irritated by the behavior, he also knows how well they work together. Besides, these battles are small and, overall, Richard knows that Lisa is supportive and on his side. After all, it is in her best interest to see him succeed and vice versa.

16

In Living Colors

Slowly, the players in this ongoing contest of wills have become comfortable in their new roles and more comfortable with each other. Perhaps as a result, Pantone's future looks increasingly robust. The once speculative projects have taken a back seat to initiatives that are more promising and that recommit the company to Larry's longtime quest for global expansion. Pantone has opened an office in Japan, expanded its commerce in China, launched a presence in India and restructured the European offices. All accomplished without investing millions and millions of dollars.

That's not enough for Richard, the apple who has clearly not fallen far from the tree. "I think my father has taken us to a certain point, and there's still more we can do under his control," he asserts. "I think there's a lot more value, opportunity and security we could create by taking Pantone to another level."

Building security, a priority for Richard, means keeping the family finances stable, even for future generations who may or may not work at Pantone. The PANTONE Language is key, which makes safe-guarding it as crucial to Richard as it is to Larry.

Larry's philosophy, which has so influenced his son, stems from his belief that there are creators and copycats, producers and parasites. When Richard broke into the color printer ink business with ColorVANTAGE® inks, he ran up against a large printer manufacturer. The printer manufacturer had threatened retailers by withholding product if they decided to carry PANTONE Printer Inks.

Larry had survived threats from big companies before, and he didn't scare easily. "You want to frighten me? Put me in a foxhole in Korea where they are shooting," he remarked. Feeling that this would constitute part of Richard's education in developing a business, father and son together went to the Department of Justice with their complaint.

Safeguarding the PANTONE Language, however, is almost an incidental cost of doing business, of spreading the Pantone word around the globe. Pantone had already established itself as an international language under Larry's watch, so why the same quest, one wonders? Richard presents the issue differently. "Pantone is actually used by a very small percentage of the population at large. Take the United States, for example. Every professional designer, marketing or corporate communications expert knows Pantone, and once you have saturated that market, where do you go?" Operating at what he refers to as the tip of the iceberg, Richard envisions greater opportunity, driving Pantone to ten percent of the potential market, a market he sees in the masses.

Establishing the PANTONE Language of Color in broader international markets affords Pantone the opportunity to generate revenue through supporting products. Products like artist materials and special color books, based on the PANTONE MATCHING SYSTEM, have generated income for years. But establishing new products would generate millions of dollars more. Items intended to shift from the professional to the consumer market and into the consumer "think color, think PANTONE" consciousness include inkjet cartridges for professional printers, photographers, design tools, color and electronic gadgets. Lisa had even produced little purses styled from PANTONE Chips.

As everyone attaches a meaning to a brand, this promotional value allows for trickle down consumerism. For instance, if Pantone makes a name in the professional printer market, the next step would be to produce ink cartridges for narrow format printers —the lower cost market. Add licensing opportunities to the mix and Pantone's value rises into a new category.

As a result, Pantone expects to drive the color market. To build broader audiences, in addition to inkjet cartridges, Pantone has already licensed monitor calibration equipment, writing instruments, stationery and more. The success of the stationery line in Japan and at the 2005 Stationery Show, for example, prompted Pantone to distribute the product in the U.S. at well-known specialty retailers like Conran's, Sam Flax, A.I. Friedman, Felissimo and numerous art material stores. "If this hits in the United States with one of the larger retailers, it will be a huge success for Pantone. We're not only talking about the notebooks but the color-coordinated markers, writing instruments, diaries, desktop accessories like staplers and tape dispensers, erasers, scissors, any item you see in a stationery or back-to-school department," says Lisa.

Vicky's consulting has introduced Pantone to clients like Verizon. Vicky and Tod Schulman, vice president of textiles, worked on a proposal to help brand the VCAST products in a similar manner to Apple's white iPod® Pantone had to come up with the right choice, the color that could be used on ancillary devices such as headphones, as well as the actual phones themselves. Taken a step further into the consumer market, the Japanese company, SoftBank, designed cell phones and offered them in an array of 20 PANTONE Colors. The screens of these phones morph all 20 colors, one after another. Additionally, the billboard advertising references the PANTONE Logo as it positions all 20 phones in a rainbow. With a market crowded with gizmos and gadgets, something as simple as a personal preference of color can give a company an edge.

Richard's quest for expansion hasn't been without its mistakes. Metamorphosing a company requires clear goals and the ability to say 'no' to many time-wasting prospects. One Internet initiative, TheRightColor.com, attempted to convince manufacturers and retailers in the housewares and furnishings arenas to work from the same PANTONE Palette. After selecting a color from the palette, it would then be displayed on each product's information tag so customers could go online to find other companies that produce matching or complementary accessories.

The idea, which has future potential, bombed. "We just kept pushing that rock up a hill," chuckles Richard. Building customer loyalty and sales through preference information, à la Amazon, sets up a whole new communication scheme with color. The timing too soon for the marketplace, the work too time-consuming, and funding complicated by investors who required part ownership in the Pantone company, Richard remains hopeful that the project will resume once Pantone extends its language into the mass market. Integrating into the consumer market on a bricks and mortar level, rather than solely a dot com level, feels more naturally aligned with everything else Pantone does.

Cementing the name PANTONE into buyers' consciousness is one of the company's newest goals. The idea is to have people associate color with the name Pantone as readily as they associate that red bull's eye logo with Target stores. So they're hitting customers where they live…literally.

For starters, if everything goes according to plan, Pantone will market and sell a range of consumer color products in a store near you soon, according to Richard, and will prove one of Pantone's mainstays, at least in the consumer mind. Years earlier, a deal between Pantone and Behr paints fell through, mainly because Larry and the owner of Behr didn't administer the project directly. Had they made a deal then, Pantone would be much farther ahead in its current consumerism game plan. "The natural progression is paint," says Richard. A deal was finally realized with Fine Paints of Europe in 2006 when Pantone launched PANTONE PAINTS based on its tried and true color formulations, along with its PAINTS + INTERIORS Color Guide in a portable fan deck format.

The consumer dominoes will fall into a PANTONE Color Universe of paints, textiles, carpeting, whatever, all using the same system. "We may have to wait for a few more people to die who are holding on to the old way," Larry concurs, but Pantone has those dominoes lined up and ready to go.

Of course, just like the corporations who seek color advice from Pantone, the company will need to know what colors to market when the time comes. Not surprisingly, Pantone holds a membership with the Color Marketing Group, an organization that gathers and provides information on color trends, culled from sources like, yes, Pantone, to all areas of manufacturing. For instance, if American Standard is producing a sink and toilet in a particular color, the manufacturer of the toilet seat or the manufacturer of bathroom accessories need to know the exact color to provide uniformity for their products.

But Pantone has its own color forecasting arm, the direct result of all those people and clients who for years asked, "What does Pantone think?" So when Staples began its B2B Division selling completely furnished offices with all the fixings, they had to turn to the PANTONE Color Forecast for up-to-the-minute color information for their desktop accessories.

For years, Pantone has shared its color trend information with the professional design audience in its PANTONE VIEW Colour Planner — a twice yearly, multi-platform forecast offering seasonal inspiration for men's, women's, active, cosmetics, interiors and industrial design. Showing off a line of new handbags on CBS TV's Sunday Morning, Bloomingdale's Fashion Director, Stephanie Soliman, explains that since the handbags are actually manufactured a year in advance, "We need to know that pink [will] be important a year later, so we trust companies like Pantone to give us direction." Similarly, when Tupperware recently wanted to update its look, the company turned to Pantone for a new palette. The consult presentation gave a viewpoint on future colors for the kitchen as well as in fashion, with a strong note about the look of colored metallics.

Forecasting fashion colors two years in advance of hitting the market can be tricky since it is not a precise science. In the past, Lee Eiseman forecasted greens morphing to turquoise as part of an ecological trend and juxtaposed it with the influence of technology, the blues on computer screens, LED readouts and other influences. Blues, bright, cobalt, indigo, then hit the runways. How did she do it? With a little help from her friends.

Twice a year, a group of nine color consultants who work with designers and design firms converge in Europe, in one of several countries where the designers reside: Spain, Holland, Italy, France,

England and the United States. Since only Lee Eiseman and Tod Schulman attend from the U.S., with Lisa as an onlooker, the meetings have remained in Europe.

David Shah, publisher of the VIEW Colour Planner book and meeting coordinator, E-mails the group with an advance date for the meeting and a reminder to come armed with opinions, facts and viewpoints. On the first day, the meeting begins early in the morning with a colorful invocation of sorts by David as he talks about what he has seen in the market to get everyone geared up. As the conversation moves around the room, it turns to themes and influences: what have they noticed sociologically, psychologically, culturally and economically? Do there seem to be trends occurring? And what colors do these happenings and trends most evoke?

The group considers the present marketplace and color climate because that will influence the upcoming palette choices. "Colors," Lisa explains, "are not in and then out. It's more of an evolution." The forecast represents a comprehensive range of the spectrum and selected palettes that are used in a variety of ways — fashion, interiors and architecture. When a color scheme is very popular, like brights, for example, it may last through several seasons. Thereafter, it generally doesn't disappear but, rather, may become muted: as saturated as before, just not as vivid.

The seasonal palettes represent moods like somber, cheerful, hopeful and the like. The group considers all palettes: bright colors, sober colors, neutrals and everything in between. All are issued in the forecast. Proportion governs how the palettes are used. "Let's say the somber colors weren't indicative of the world or a country, that color palette might still be used, for instance, on a very up-market product or as a base with brightly colored accents," explains Lisa. The juxta-position of colors remains the important factor. This also explains how different colors appear in different parts of the same market. Brighter, more youthful colors may show up in popular merchandise stores, whereas a designer may give the nod to a more reserved color.

As each member relates certain imagery, patterns occur. During one session, the Italian representative talked about how Incredible Hulk green just wouldn't go away. In a show-and-tell, he displayed other packaging that employed the color green. Though he, like the others, disliked Incredible Hulk green, the fact that green appeared as often as it did clearly signaled the need to pay attention to the color's importance in the marketplace, thus extending its life. The Spanish representative presented color boards with mood palettes, using photographs and pictures swiped from magazines as a visual aid.

Lisa recalls one particular season when the member from London began to discuss the city's overwhelming amount of con-struction — the clanking hammers, the teeth-rattling drills, and overall inescapable noise. The situation had become so bad that the British Opera House proposed to play continual music to overshadow the daylong clamor. The two Americans piped in with the fact that New York City's Mayor Bloomberg had reported the same condition. The result of the discussion was a plan that incorporated workmanship, craft and the colors related to metals and a hammered metal looks.

After a morning of give and take, bantering, discussions, agreements and disagreements, colors are chosen by the group members. The afternoon session begins with grouping the colors based on similarities and assigning themes to the color palettes. By day's end, all can walk away with 46 to 50 forecasted colors, which are then turned over to a design studio to create the visual.

Many of the ideas that go into the VIEW Colour Planner become the basis of planning for fashion designers, product development, home furnishings and large brand apparel manufacturers like Liz Claiborne and Jones New York. As compared to the late 1980s, when only three percent of those businesses polled said they had based decisions on a color consultancy, today nearly all fashion-related industries rely on color trend forecasting to get it right. Even retailers who create and produce private label brands, as do Neiman Marcus and Nordstrom, need to keep ahead of the trends and use the forecasts.

Designers, the contributing force behind the palette forecasts, have stepped up to lend their designs and thoughts for each season's FASHION COLOR REPORT. Each season for the fashion show, 12,000 narrow format, full-color spiral booklets are produced by Pantone and given away. For fall 2006, young designer Zac Posen offered his sketch for a sultry gown in Bijou Blue (PANTONE 18-3921; C:88, M:71, Y:25, K:3) with this philosophy, "There is nothing sexier and more real than navy and jet…moody and rich."The palette attested to dependable colors: neutral, earthy, smoky, sexy and richly saturated with names like Apple Cinnamon, Golden Ochre, Mineral Red, Vetiver, Bijou Blue, Purple Magic and Red Mahogany, to name a few. Each season's selected designer names run the alphabet from Alice Roi to Zac Posen. The colors and designs float to market on a magic carpet.

Life, however, doesn't always cooperate with the forecast. In 2001, as every year before, the major palettes had been set along with a discussion of their themes. When disaster stuck on 9/11, a somber mood blanketed the world. Clearly, cheerful and bright palettes would not take hold with the U.S. public. Instead, as a result of the tragedy, people wanted to be surrounded by red, white and blue. In fact, Pantone received so many calls with regard to the flag that they standardized the colors and offered them free of charge. Since included among the VIEW Colour Planner palettes were various reds and blues, the staff, under Lee Eiseman's guidance, pulled together more appropriate colors into a "Heritage" palette.

Admittedly not the only forecaster of color trends, particularly in Europe, Pantone remains the best identifier of color, helping others like the Color Marketing Group and the Color Association to cross-reference their selections. The textile division maintains some 2,000 colors in the system and, much to Larry's consternation, inventories enough swatches for each color reference at Pantone.

On the heels of the success with the PANTONE VIEW Colour

Planner, Lisa's department introduced a smaller, portable, more targeted version for the home furnishings market — The PANTONE VIEW Home Planner. Produced annually, the book offers similar color palettes and color harmonies, and the CMYK values of each should someone want to mimic those colors in any print medium, whether packaging or catalog. Each year the department tries to improve the product based on testing. Color strips, color cards and a cross-reference to the color system for housewares manufacturers (think Dyson and Miele colored vacuum cleaners) have all been added since inception.

Taking its own advice, Pantone's Consumer Products Division, headed up by Lisa, focuses on developing products that utilize this core competency — i.e., its expertise in color — into consumer goods. For starters, under Lisa's direction with an assist from Vicky in the color consulting department, Pantone launched the first color program for the firm Colorcalm, an ambient media producer, as well as the launch of dinner and glassware rimmed with PANTONE Swatches through Fishs Eddy in October 2004. On sale in New York's Museum of Modern Art Design Store and Fishs Eddy, the PANTONE Collection offers seasonally selected colors from its current fashion-forward color trend collections.

The dinnerware collection, along with the rest of the products that Pantone plans to introduce, provides Pantone with the perfect venue to educate the consumer on color. Along with its characteristic numerical tag, each color carries an identifying name and description.

NAME THAT TONE

Revealing the seasonal fashion colors has developed into a celebratory occasion. Fashion, graphic design, architects, beauty and entertainment leaders helped label the colors on the spring 2000 list, naming those that most inspired them.

Cosmetic mogul Aerin Lauder named PANTONE 7451 FLIP FLOP PURPLE.

Renowned architect I.M. Pei dubbed PANTONE 7531 ICARUS.

Creative Director Simon Doonan Of Barney's designated PANTONE 7408 as CHICA CHICA BOOM (for Carmen Miranda).

New York City Ballet master Peter Martins called PANTONE 7417 NEO-MEXICO.

Industrial Designer Mar Newson termed PANTONE 7488 SOILENT GREEN.

Every season will bring with it a new color palette, an updated look and new informational material on color.

The Housewares Show has created the perfect venue for Pantone to display actual product using PANTONE Colors. The booth, surrounded by eight giant panels, each portraying one of the eight color palettes for the season, becomes the backdrop for handpicked manufacturers to show their wares. Pantone has worked with Homer Laughlin China Co., makers of Fiestaware, Le Creuset cookware

Pfaltzgraff tableware, Kitchenaid and Lifetime Brands, a company with multiple brand name products. PANTONE Color Watch, as it is called, has caught the attention of major trade magazines like HFN (Home Furnishings News), who call to find out which companies Pantone will be displaying at the show. This has helped Pantone position itself in the home furnishings market while giving the man ufacturer double exposure, a win-win situation if there ever was one.

The next step? Perhaps the consumer electronics arena with the PANTONE Plastics Color System™. Vicky and Tod worked on color boards and color combinations for a jazzier, fashion-oriented, multi-colored Jabra Bluetooth earphone launched at the spring 2006 Consumer Electronics Show (CES). Since then, they have added PANTONE Color flash drives for Mac and PC.

From the dinner table, Pantone has extended its reach to con-summers with its expanding home collection. In early 2006, Pantone inaugurated a new bed and bath collection in Japan, including sheets and pillowcases, towels, area rugs, floor mats, shower curtains and robes. The collection, created by Pantone's winning design team, which includes Barbara Devries from Calvin Klein and Jane Harkness, former president of Coach who started Barney's Co-Op, once again reflects the company's colorful philosophy by incorporat-ing the Home Color Forecast trends. Retailed by the trendy depart-ment store, LOFT, which first launched the stationery line, it targets an audience of young, hip, fashion-savvy consumers aged twenty to forty-five. Next step for the road-tested collection…the United States.

The people who once only formulated color systems and reference materials for designers did not initially have experience in making these end-use products. But the formerly genderless Pantone consumer has turned into a sea of styles, tastes and needs.

With an intense learning process facing her, Lisa has created a completely new department to employ design services and to market different disciplines. "We had to retool our thinking," she explains. The whole aspect of marketing to the consumer has taken on a life of its own. Its mission: to create succinct new messages elucidating the advantages of owning a PANTONE Product.

Whether stationery or track shoes, each product standing alone won't get the job done. However, as Richard contends, these are not meant to be isolated businesses. Each builds on the next…part of a bigger strategy to build brand awareness and educate the consumer-at-large to communicate color by numbers.

Perhaps the consumer's level of color awareness can reach a point as noted in "Reno Dakota," a song by indie rock group, The Magnetic Fields.

> *You know you enthrall ne*
> *and yet you don't call me.*
> *It's making me blue,*
> *PANTONE 292*

Indeed, Pantone has already become its own language among designers. They don't just speak in PANTONE to communicate job specifics, they also refer to specific colors to communicate state-of-mind and more.

> *When Marcia saw my new pair of designer shoes, she was 355 [green with envy].*
> *When I broke that dish, my father went 185 [red with rage].*

Clearly, a large part of the PANTONE Product appeal lies in its color trendiness — a Pantone specialty. Consultancy is Vicky's area of expertise, and she and Lisa work hand in hand. Over the years, more and more companies have approached Pantone to discuss their color needs and validate their color choices, whether for company logos or packaging. Awareness of Pantone's expertise has become staggering.

"I'm always surprised by the different kinds of companies that call us instead of calling independent consultants," declares Vicky, whose imposing list of clients ranges from Jabra and Verizon to H&R Block to Tupperware. Indeed, every conceivable consumer product and packaging concern relies on Pantone for its color because "we have the ability to look at things from so many different vantage points when we offer a consultancy program." Collaborating in 2005, for example, Timex and *Glamour* magazine retained Pantone to identify and validate fashion colors for a trendy new line of Indiglo watches.

Pantone's calling card, the chip, has made its way into the consumer market — and consciousness — in more artistic fashion.

The "Flight Stool" project, a limited edition collection of stools executed by Vicky, "brings the iconic PANTONE Chip — universally recognized by artists and designers — to life in three dimensions," explains Jay Osgerby, co-principal of the design team Barber Osgerby. "It is the merging of a graphic language with a functional object in a way that has not been seen since the Pop Art era. Art meets object in an interesting tension between the graphic and the real." Seen gracing the stylish windows of Barney's Madison Avenue flagship store, the colorful array of stools, each with its identifying PANTONE Number and signed by Larry[37] when purchased, bolsters the idea that color communicates our sense of uniqueness and individuality.

Barney's Creative Director, Simon Doonan, finds the surreal, wacky stools a perfect color and design fit. In August 2005, he paired sculptural piles of the stools with the latest fall collections in his windows and gave Pantone its due. The window front sign read: *Pantone, the company that designers turn to for color expertise now offers product for every aspect of your life.*

"Who ever thought the PANTONE Chip could become a piece of furniture?" asks Doonan in a matter-of-fact way. "The whole thing is very groovy!"

Originally created for the Freedom Brewing Co. in Central London, this high-end, limited edition has been featured in two London exhibits — one at the Design Museum and another at The

---

[37] *In the 2005 London exhibits, designers Barber and Ogersby signed editions of the stools.*

Blue Gallery. It remains part of the permanent collection of the Victoria & Albert Museum.

PANTONE Chips have taken on a life of their own, it would seem. Famous fashion designer Calvin Klein places a PANTONE Chip next to his coffee maker to ensure that he receives his coffee blended with just the right amount of milk.[38] At Ben & Jerry's, cooked brownies must fall between PANTONE 469 Rich Brown chip and PANTONE 490 Purplish Brown chip to be deemed acceptable.[39]

With the advent of synthetic dyes, advanced color printing, color cinematography and television, our world of color has expanded. Since Medieval times, when a shade or two of blue (from the indigo mineral and the woad plant) was acceptable, today hundreds of hues and shades that run from dark to light and blue/green to blue/violet complement our lives. Of its 2,000 plus color palette considered for fashion, home interiors and electronic display, Pantone has created over 200 variations of blue alone.

The company has come a long way from the days when it was just another printing company. Each day, Larry Herbert drives to work from Manhattan's Upper East Side through the Lincoln Tunnel to Carlstadt, New Jersey. He parks his car in spot number one, next to the entrance, walks up the stairs to the second floor and presses a code to enter the offices.

---

[38] *Marsh, Lisa, "House of Klein: Fashion, Controversy and a Business Obsession," Wiley & Sons, Hoboken, NJ, Sept. 2003.*
[39] *Fass, Allison, "The Color of Money," Forbes Magazine, November 24, 2003.*

Each day, though the pressures have shifted over the years from infringement cases and lack of money to the business' internal workings, Larry challenges his Pantone team to maintain a sense of urgency. "I keep telling them 'I don't buy green bananas anymore.'" He's concerned about the deals being made, as well as the ongoing research because of how quickly technology passes. "All the progress," he says, "that occurred between 1900 and 1990 has been surpassed during 1990 to 2003."

Though the picture has changed, the problem-solving remains the same to this day. Ink and its components require constant attention. When the Coach Leather Company brought two leather samples to Pantone to create a color tolerance, the swatches unfortunately differed greatly in color. Pantone worked on fine-tuning the chasm and achieved an acceptable tolerance level within two days. However, each time the color strips are printed on different stocks, coated or uncoated, and viewed in different lights, variances occur leaving colors to appear lighter, duller, darker or dirtier. It took another six more months of fine-tuning until it all looked the same.

Pantone custom matches ice cream cones for Kellogg's and creates an acceptable tolerance in terms of the lightest and darkest cone colors. They do the same for Nabisco crackers and apply the color to plastic so workers can determine which crackers don't make the grade.

It would seem that Larry has color-matched just about everything you can imagine. He even charted color gemstones — rubies, sapphires and emeralds — for a GIA (Gemological Institute of America) appraiser. The appraiser had come up with the idea of matching the colors of gemstones through a code number to facilitate replacement. Say a customer came into a jeweler having lost a ruby from a necklace. A jeweler would need to match the stone, which required receiving packets of stones from dealers in the right size and shape. The shade, however, always presented a problem and made the process time-consuming. Having a gemstone chart that identified gem colors by number would simplify that phase.

To create this gemstone code, Larry was handed a row of rubies placed on white paper and asked to match them. Just as he had done with glasses of red and white wine for the California Wine Association, Larry replicated the gem gradings by printing on plastic with specially formulated inks, a method he had previously devised while working with the Levine Brothers' ad agency on fashion display light boxes.

The appraiser marketed the resulting books, enabling jewelers to match the remaining stones and call in the order by number, saving an enormous amount of time.

Problem-solving had even reached beyond printing and color matching and into the foray of inks. When opened ink cans resulted in a skin developing along the top, hours were wasted trying to remove the dried layer of ink. Larry's simple solution: turn the can upside down and work from the bottom, leaving the last half-inch in every can. When press ready time took too long, Larry realized that the ink temperature was to blame. He sat with his technicians, decided to build an oven to maintain the correct press temperature for the inks. "Set it up and put the inks in the night before, so they are warm when you get in." This saved an hour-and-a-half on make-ready every day.

Larry may have given up the presidency of Pantone, but the company will always carry his mark of distinction. With his dry sense of humor, he points out "I'm not just an old fossil here; I actually know what I'm talking about." He still wants people to use him as a resource. Larry's expansive office suite, where everyone must pass on his or her way to work, lies between the locked door and the rest of the offices. As he settles behind his glass top desk, cleared of clutter save for his phone, he has his coffee and a buttered Kaiser roll. A massive fish tank filled with Comet fish rescued from his former East Hampton summer residence sits to his left like moving wall art.

The fish remain as a reminder of one of Larry's more challenging color matching jobs. Koi breeders separate fish by color as early as three weeks old and, for serious breeders and collectors, colors run the gamut of the rainbow. Breeding for color is done by selection, with rare combinations commanding hundreds of thousands of dollars. Larry received a carton filled with goldfish swimming in a plastic container half-filled with water. Immediately, he ran out to buy a tank and food to take care of the fish. When it came time to match the various colors, he scooped out a fish and placed it in a jar of water. Not wanting to harm any of the fish, the process required eyeball

251

precision. To recreate the iridescent quality of the colors, Larry printed the results on a coated stock and superimposed a screen to illustrate the effect of scales.

Beyond the fish tank are a sofa and coffee table and his private bathroom. Positioned to his right, a mini conference table and chairs sit poised beneath a portrait of Santa Claus fashioned from colorful PANTONE Chips. Pantone has clearly been good to him.

Larry has never taken his success for granted. He sits on the boards and actively participates with the American Film Institute and the New York City Ballet. While he pays attention to his lifestyle, he also attends to those in need and receives accolades for the contributions he's made that have supported worthy institutions and causes and bettered the lives of others. That's the deal he made with Elsie Williamson those many years ago.

Perhaps Larry could not have predicted this future, but he made the right choices. From the instant he grabbed hold of that rainbow's tail, he went for the ride of his life. He is, after all, the undeniable King of Color.

17

Afterword from Lawrence Herbert

When I first wrote *The King of Color* to narrate my story of Pantone, I didn't anticipate there would be another chapter. But, then again, from the very beginning of my life at Pantone as a pressman and color-matcher at age 27, I never imagined that Pantone would grow into the company it is today in part because of my questioning nature. I wondered why a color didn't appear the same each and every time it was mixed and printed. Though a theoretically straightforward idea, the process of standardizing formulas from pigments and chemicals proved lengthy and complicated. Without these standardized formulas, though, a drop of any additional color or foreign substance could change an ink formula drastically, rendering a print job useless. Painstaking work, combined with precision and control, created a world of difference for the printing industry. It was satisfying and worthwhile once we could duplicate color simply by a standard formula. For me, though, that wasn't enough. My dream was to own the company; I couldn't possibly create something and leave it behind. I knew that the Color Matching System would be successful and that to own the company was vital. It took some doing, but I managed to buy Pantone.

During the growth of Pantone from a printing press to an international commodity, I became immersed in everything Pantone. I had to push forward, and failure wasn't an option. I had to keep the day to day business going, and I had to continue to expand into unknown territories. This was a labor of love and how I made my living. I was very much an entrepreneur…even before I knew what that meant… a pioneer.

Working left very little time to look back at any of my accomplishments. I just didn't think about it. It was only when business threw me a curveball that I needed to take stock, make that assessment, and then figure out how to move forward. This happened to me a few times during my tenure at Pantone. As a young pressman in 1956, to owning the company less than 6 years later and beyond, I would encounter many trials and tribulations along the path to the company becoming the authority on color. Pantone Press, once one of many commercial printers, formed a culture that would invade all aspects of our lives.

While the 60s were spent developing books for the Matching System, our main product, Pantone began to investigate ways to license the system for use with other products, the natural fit being the art and design industry. Here's where we took our first blow. We were still a young company breaking into new realms, as were some of the companies with which we dealt. When licensees' payments weren't forthcoming, and contracts were breached, our cash reserves took a hit from the lawsuits. By the early 70s, the company's profits began to decline even though we continued our outreach into new markets.

This drain prompted my decision: I needed capital to keep going. So, in April 1970 I set up a "Regulation A" public offering of 100,000 shares at $3.00 per share. By today's standards, that's a pittance. But, for a small company like mine, it was the difference between life and death.

These lawsuits were funded mostly by our first two years of profits. In the end, it was worth every penny to protect the Pantone name, trademark, copyright, formulas and expression of color. The lawsuit that brought this about occurred against an artist materials company shockingly named Para-Tone. They had printed a color comparison sheet that was distributed to artist materials dealers in competition to our product. The problem, as proven in court, was that their colors were extracted directly from the Pantone Matching System. They were even so bold as to indicate, on the sheet itself, which Pantone color numbers they used. The final decision, in favor of Pantone, boosted our visibility in the marketplace, put us on solid ground "not to be messed with" and immediately won us a pending licensing agreement with 3M. The trade press was all over this and from then on the scales began to tip our way; things got a little easier. Afterward, I remember seeing a cartoon, a David vs. Goliath-depiction that was published in one of the trade magazines. It illustrated a little guy wearing a crown of colors, throwing stones at a giant. I got a good laugh from this.

But, I'm also not the kind of guy to rest on my laurels. It's my nature to pursue excellence and to expand my horizons.

I'm a problem-solver, an answer man. If a problem arose, I needed answers. I always looked for ways to maintain quality control for our clients and vendors. I investigated the issue until I found a solution. Sometimes, though, we had to learn from our mistakes, our most significant having occurred in the early 1970s when faulty Matching System books were shipped to Australia. Apparently, one printer's client chose a color from these flawed PMS books, and, the printer, having used the appropriate formula, ended up with a completely different color on the final job. The client refused the job, of course. We immediately shipped new books and reimbursed the printer for the money he lost on the job so he wouldn't sue the ink manufacturer. Here's how the mistake occurred: while the Matching System book printing job was being set up on the presses and the ink was poured into the ink fountain, a drop or so of the ink splashed onto the roller. So, while the press was running, this additional bit of ink created books with out-of-whack color, color that didn't match the formulas. This could have become a bigger tragedy if it hadn't come to our attention. For my part, I resolved that this could never happen again. So, we sought a solution and figured out how to block the print roller from accidental splashes while the ink was being poured. It was one case where we didn't even need to spend a lot of money to build any fancy machinery…just be inventive. To be sure the process worked, I increased inspections during and after a press run. Funny, though, I always wondered what happened to the other incorrectly printed books we shipped. I guess we'll never know.

While still a public company and under the watchful eye and tight fist of the Pantone Board of Directors, my once private company felt like an open book: everything came into question. It never stopped me from making decisions, but answering to someone else, especially about the everyday minutiae, was time-consuming. Plus, the cost of producing an annual report was obscenely high. I finally reached the point where I no longer wanted my company handled in this manner, and I wasn't about to walk away from something so important to me. I'm a leader, not a follower.

During this time, too, the economy tightened its grip, resulting in rising unemployment, double-digit inflation, and skyrocketing interest rates. This and the previously mentioned lawsuits drained our coffers, which is why we had gone public. People began manipulating stocks by buying, running up the price, and then getting out. Wall Street ethics and controls just didn't seem to exist. Pantone, too, lost ground: the $8 or $9 per share dropped all the way to $.60 per share. Advisors pressed me to buy back the stock. So, with help, I recovered 100% of my company and my sanity by 1977.

Color is central to our business and one thing you can expand upon. Day-Glo colors stole the scene in the 60s; we instituted a color system for fabric dyes and digital coloring, to name a few of our color innovations. Many of the initiatives and licenses began while my kids, Lisa, Richard, and Victoria joined the company back in 1974 as summertime employees.

The three permanently established themselves in the company, each working in a different capacity. Each seemed to fall into a natural zone. With the coming of the digital age, Richard's degree in 'all things computer' occurred at just the right time; Lisa, the go-getter, dominated the marketing and licensing with her creative ideas; and, Vicky fielded all sorts of inquiries, knowing just who could handle any specific issue, and worked with the Pantone Color Institute. She also had her finger on the pulse of our archives. I put my faith in these kids to inject some new blood into the company and come up with innovative ideas and initiatives. But, like a father, a boss, a business owner, I hovered over every detail, driving them and everyone else nuts. Nevertheless, their efforts and initiatives pressed us into a global force. Richard inserted himself right away into the research and development of the Professional Color System through its production and launch, then took on the textile color system and the Mode Information deal, an online forecast trending resource. As part of his grooming to become president, he ran global sales and marketing and implemented product development initiatives that increased revenue. Pantone stretched beyond its borders as a resource to graphic designers and into the mass market of everyday goods. Even singer Katie Perry donned the 2018 Color of the Year on her hair…Ultra Violet. Though Pantone is not in the business of hair dye, when asked what color she would next choose, Perry commented, "Just pick a Pantone color."

Afterword

ULTRA VIOLET, THE PANTONE COLOR OF 2018

Since the Phoenicians discovered purple, it clothed regal figures. Rendered from rare dead snails, the natural dye known as Tyrian purple was difficult to procure and costly to render. Thus, it could only be acquired by the wealthiest clientele. Throughout history, it remained associated with royalty, including Queen Elizabeth II, who was seen wearing the electric shade just after its announcement in December 2017.

Our initiatives in licensing, directed by Lisa, reached into just about every avenue. You could see our brand on phone cases, beer cans, children's books about color, makeup and makeup color palettes, bedding linens, household paints, and even a hotel in Brussels. Licensing initiatives gradually gave way to more consulting and collaboration.

When I began writing the original version of the book, *The King of Color*, as part of my legacy, I hadn't yet determined that I would sell the company. Like others, I had thought all along that Pantone would remain a family business even after I left, but I had been approached with the idea of selling several times over the years Pantone had become the 'go-to' color company on which all others relied. More than that, though, the Pantone Color System was considered a unique form of communication and, because of this, many companies, individuals and blogs sprung up to proselytize the psychology, theory, and meaning of colors, and how to use them. The Color Matching System, which assigned numbers to each color, eventually gave names to some of the colors when we expanded into the consumer audience. Pantone continued its growth beyond graphic design and into the consumer field with consulting, licensing and the Color of the Year, but we always maintained our reach into the trade.

The Color of the Year program was an entity unto itself: It bridged the gap between the trade clientele and the mass consumer. Though the Color of the Year program began in 2000 at the Pantone Color Institute, it actually had been something that Leatrice Eiseman initiated in 1986 to research color trends. Now, the Institute continues its direction under Lea.

So, with all that was happening, why did I think about selling the company? The topic did come up every few years, mostly by me, but the timing had to be right. When Pantone finally grew into a worldwide trade and consumer name, I began giving it more serious thought; I was past any retirement age and initiatives, which were now all over the map, became increasingly more costly. Plus, the company's value had risen. Too, my charities took on a greater meaning. And, with Richard as president of the company, it freed me to spend even more time on charity work, my alma mater topping the list.

Years ago, I had been approached by Dick Bennett at Hofstra University to join the Board of Trustees. I joined the Board of Directors in 1979, became Vice Chairman of the Board in 1984, and left in 1985 just before my term ended in 1986. In 1986, remember, Pantone

THE PANTONE MATCHING SYSTEM

The Pantone Matching System consists of the original swatches for printing on paper, either coated or uncoated stock; Pantone metallic colors; the four-color process guide, or Pantone CMYK, and the Color Bridge, a side by side comparison of PMS colors and four-color process colors. Pantone entered the world of fashion, home and interior with its Textile guides. Next, a Pantone Plastics selector for opaque and transparent colors evolved. All were answers to a growing need in the marketplace.

Color Institute was initiated, though not formally. Lea Eiseman, who became the head of the Institute, had initially consulted with us at the time and helped in launching it. The name came about during a launch luncheon with Henry Rogers of Rogers & Cowan. Someone, I can't remember who, used the word "institute" and it stuck, officially becoming the Pantone Color Institute.

Though the Institute wasn't to be permanently housed at Hofstra, I continued my support of their work in the area of communication. The School of Communication was founded in 1995 and on October 30, 2013, in a formal gathering, to my great delight, it was re-named after me, the Lawrence Herbert School of Communication.

At the ceremony, the Dean of the School of Communication referred to me as "one of the founding fathers of the age of communication." He recalled this historical sequence of communication events: in 1995, Apple produced the Mac and the Apple computers; Amazon appeared and only sold books online; three years later, Google came on the scene followed by Facebook another six years later. They all initiated a means of communication in a new age just as I had provided a valuable tool: a practical communication standardization of the spectrum.

This was a crowning achievement for me, and it was backed by an impressive list of awards bestowed upon me over the years: the Alumni Achievement Award, Distinguished Service Award, and Alumnus of the Year Award, Honorary Doctor of Humane Letters, and the establishment of the Lawrence Herbert Distinguished Professorship Award. In May 2013, before the name change convocation, I was honored at the 17th Annual Hofstra Gala and referred to as Dr. Lawrence Herbert, Class of '51. More importantly, below my name was the word "inventor."

Also dear to my heart was the New York City Ballet and the American Film Institute. In 1985, my daughter, Lisa, chose to go to the ballet for her birthday. So, I bought an opening-night table for her. That night I happened upon my friend Earle Mack who sat on the Board of the Ballet. Well, next thing I knew, I was on the Board of Trustees in 1986 and began fundraising for the underwriting of ballet productions. This occurred during Peter Martins' accomplished leadership of the NYC Ballet. When Peter Martins left, I also decided it was time to quit the board. I was already a resident of Florida by 2006 and had begun to fundraise and underwrite performances for the Miami City Ballet. My first production commitment, by the way, was "Carnival of the Animals," originally performed by the New York City Ballet in 2003. This time, in Florida, I had the pleasure to welcome 400 kids who would otherwise never see a ballet and, after the performance, the kids flooded the lobby to say 'hello' while a woman with her granddaughter approached to thank me.

For me, there is life in the performing arts, an immediate pleasure from every move and sound. Balanchine used to say that if you don't like his steps, you could always listen to the music. Then, there was my involvement in the American Film Institute (AFI). Back in 1986, Henry Rogers (Rogers & Cowan) sat on its Board of Directors and felt that AFI needed an infusion of new blood, people outside the industry with different viewpoints. Ironically, when Ted Turner began colorizing movies, he used the Pantone System, and people thought that I had done the work. Of course, I hadn't. After 30 years on the Board of Directors and Trustees of the AFI, I retired. By the way, my son, Loren, graduated from AFI and was met with a standing ovation after the screening of his graduate film.

It has always been my great pleasure to go where help is needed. My charities also include the Alzheimer's Foundation for research in early-onset Alzheimer's in women, the Palm Beach Police Foundation and a variety of other charities in support of veterans.

I sold Pantone in 2007 because I felt it needed new wings. I wasn't abandoning my child; I was giving her in marriage. The time was right according to members of the board, and with the guidance of Goldman Sachs we set up a management committee. When I revealed my plan to the kids, they weren't surprised. Lisa, who hadn't been privy to my plan beforehand, knew the business was doing well, and she understood high brand value. After the sale, Lisa remained at Pantone until 2013 and then left to spend more time with her family.

Richard, too, remained on board, but only for a brief period. I know he would have preferred to maintain Pantone as a family business, but he understood the favorable and robust climate for mergers and acquisitions at that time.

Responsibility for a prospectus and presentations to prospective buyers went to Lisa for marketing, Richard on technologies, and Billy Chien for financials. Richard also narrated the book. The target strategy began with companies with which we had a relationship. These included Adobe, ink manufacturers, printing companies, and X-Rite. When all was said and done, in August 2007, we had an agreement with X-Rite for the purchase of Pantone.

I recall that when I had to inform the Pantone staff about the sale of the company, emptiness followed. I had known these people for a long time; they became family. Fortunately, some remained on staff.

Before the transition took place, I had already made Florida my permanent residence, but I came into the office every few weeks then and during the transition period. It's hard for someone like me to say goodbye and just walk away.

By 2012, X-Rite agreed to be acquired by the Danaher Corporation but to remain independent.

COLOR TECHNOLOGY PROVIDER
X-RITE INC. (NASDAQ: XRIT), OWNER OF THE WIDELY
USED PANTONE COLOR SYSTEM, HAS AGREED TO BE
ACQUIRED BY CONGLOMERATE
DANAHER CORP. (NYSE: DHR)
- By 24/7 Wall St.
https://www.marketwatch.com/story/x-rite-acquired-by-danaher-
xrit-dhr-2012-04-10

I do believe that the sale benefitted the future of Pantone. The Pantone Matching System will always be around, just as the telephone, television, and the Internet. It will just have to transition with the times.

Pantone colors still run through my veins; that's the reason I wrote this book.

"I prefer living in color."

— *David Hockney*